Cisco Networking Academy Program:
Fundamentals of Web Design
Design Journal and Course Project Workbook

Cisco Systems, Inc.

Cisco Networking Academy Program

Xenia Giese

Alexandra Holmes

Sponsored by Adobe Systems, Inc.

Cisco Press

Published by:
Cisco Press
201 West 103rd Street
Indianapolis, Indiana 46290   USA

Cisco Networking Academy Program:
Fundamentals of Web Design
Design Journal and Course Project Workbook

Cisco Systems, Inc.

Cisco Networking Academy Program

Xenia Giese

Alexandra Holmes

Sponsored by Adobe Systems, Inc.

Published by:
Cisco Press
201 West 103rd Street
Indianapolis, Indiana 46290   USA

Printed in the United States of America   1 2 3 4 5 6 7 8 9 0

First Printing   March 2002

Library of Congress Cataloging-in-Publication Number: 2001087347

ISBN: 1-58713-083-1

Trademark Acknowledgments

Warning and Disclaimer

Feedback Information

At Cisco Press, our goal is to create in-depth technical books of the highest quality and value. Each book is crafted with care and precision, undergoing rigorous development that involves the unique expertise of members from the professional technical community.

Readers' feedback is a natural continuation of this process. If you have any comments regarding how we could improve the quality of this book, or otherwise alter it to better suit your needs, you can contact us through e-mail at networkingacademy@ciscopress.com. Please make sure to include the book title and ISBN in your message.

We greatly appreciate your assistance.

Publisher	John Wait
Editor-in-Chief	John Kane
Executive Editor	Carl Lindholm
Cisco Systems Management	Michael Hakkert
	Tom Geitner
	William Warren
Editor	Shannon Gross
Production Manager	Patrick Kanouse
Senior Project Editor	Sheri Cain
Development Editor	Katherine Pendergast
Copy Editor	Douglas Lloyd
Technical Editors	Sarah Gross
	Susan Sands
Cover Designer	Louisa Klucznik
Editorial Assistant	Sarah Kimberly

About the Authors

Xenia Giese, World Organization of Webmasters (WOW) Certified Web Designer Apprentice, has been working in the Internet and Multimedia fields for more than five years as a web master, graphic designer, and project manager in Europe and the U.S. Currently, Xenia is a project manager for Cisco Networking Academy's Curriculum Development Team. She is also the recipient of a Multimedia Newcomer Award in her hometown of Aachen, Germany.

Alexandra Holmes, World Organization of Webmasters (WOW) Certified Web Designer Apprentice, is a technical writer for Compuware Corporation. She earned her Ph.D at King's College London. Currently, Alexandra is writing and editing curriculum for Cisco Networking Academy's Curriculum Development Team.

About the Technical Reviewers

Sarah Gross is Principal for Peachbrain Art and Entertainment, a New York-based multimedia group dedicated to providing interactive media to the fine arts community. She also acts as Creative Director and New York representative for Ninjacat Multimedia, an award-winning multimedia group specializing in new media, from concept to creation. Sarah holds a Bachelor's degree in Digital Media Studies from the University of Denver and has assumed the roles of Multimedia Developer, Creative Director, Producer, and Principal during her career in new media.

Susan Sands, CIW, iNet+, MCP, CNE, is a freelance web designer/trainer. Her experience includes co-authoring a series of training manuals, online course materials, and websites. Susan serves as an adjunct faculty member at Moraine Valley Community College. This review is dedicated to her two daughters, Michelle (age 11) and Jacqueline (age 8).

Dedication

Xenia Giese dedicates this book to her parents.

Alexandra Holmes dedicates this book to her mother.

Acknowledgments

First of all, we want to thank Alex Belous, Matthias Giessler, and Vito Amato for their tremendous ongoing support of the Fundamentals of Web Design curriculum. Their vision laid the groundwork for this book. Without their ongoing help and commitment to the Cisco Networking Academy Program, this book would not have been possible.

We would also like to acknowledge the curriculum development team at the Cisco Networking Academy for their support throughout this process.

Finally, we want to thank the technical reviewers, Sarah Gross and Susan Sands, for their careful review and suggestions as well as our editors, Shannon Gross and Katie Pendergast, for their guidance throughout the process.

Table of Contents

Introduction

Cisco Networking Academy Program: Fundamentals of Web Design, Design Journal and Course Project Workbook supplements your classroom and laboratory experience with the Cisco Networking Academy Program.

The *Design Journal and Course Project Workbook* provides you with additional material related to web design. This book closely follows the style and format of the Cisco curriculum. In addition, the chapters of this book correlate with those of the curriculum. Finally, this book is complemented by a CD-ROM, which contains lab material, self-assessment tools, reference materials, and productivity tools.

This book contains labs that take you step-by-step through the process of creating a website. This website is the course project for the Cisco Networking Academy Program. You learn how to create a template, logo, header, flowchart, navigational buttons, and style sheet for a website. Then you learn how to set up pages, assemble the site, and publish it.

This book also contains focus questions to test your understanding of design concepts and review questions to help you prepare for exams. It also contains discovery exercises that are designed to help you discover how design concepts are applied to real-world web-sites. These discovery exercises will create a scrapbook of design elements and code that you can use when designing your own website.

The Goal of This Book

The goal of this book is to guide you through creating a website and help you review concepts and technologies discussed in the *Cisco Networking Academy Program: Fundamentals of Web Design Companion Guide* (ISBN 1-58713-066-1). It is designed for use in conjunction with the Cisco Networking Academy Program curriculum.

This Book's Audience

The *Cisco Networking Academy Program: Fundamentals of Web Design, Design Journal and Course Project Workbook* is an effective resource for anyone who wants to learn how to create a website. The main audience for this book is students in high schools, community colleges, and four-year institutions. This book is designed for use in the classroom as the course project for the Fundamentals of Web Design curriculum. Students are also encouraged to use the material gathered during discovery exercises for future projects after completion of the curriculum.

This Book's Features

Many of this book's features will help you review design concepts, create a design scrapbook, and create the course project:

- **Focus questions**—These short answer or essay questions will help you focus on the important concepts covered in the Fundamentals of Web Design curriculum and Companion Guide.

- **Discovery exercises**—These exercises are designed to help you discover how design concepts are applied to real-world websites. When you complete all the discovery exercises, you will have created a scrapbook of design elements and code examples that you can then use as inspiration for your websites.

- **Labs**—The majority of labs will be used to create the course project: the Washington High School website. You will also download useful applications and collect material for your portfolio.

- **Review questions**—Each chapter has 10-20 review questions. The questions reinforce the concepts discussed in the *Companion Guide* and curriculum and can be used to prepare for in-class exams.

About the CD-ROM

This book is complemented by a CD-ROM, which contains lab material, self-assessment tools, reference materials, and productivity tools. These materials effectively support self-directed learning by allowing you to engage in your learning and skill building. Additionally, these learning reference materials provide the following:

- An easy-to-use graphical user interface

- Frequent interaction with content

- Printable reference material

- Interactive self-assessment tools

- Lab materials including the necessary assets

CD-ROM Hardware and Software Requirements

Processor   PC Minimum required: 166 MHz Pentium

PC Recommended: 266 MHz or greater Pentium

Macintosh: 150 MHz PowerPC

Memory   PC Minimum required: 32 MB

PC Recommended: 64 MB

Macintosh: 64 MB

OS   PC Minimum required: Windows 95

PC Recommended: Windows 98 or Windows NT 4.0

Macintosh: Mac OS 8.0

Monitor & Video Card

PC Minimum required: 800 x 600 resolution

PC Recommended: 1024 x 768 resolution

Macintosh: 1024 x 768 resolution

Software

Internet Explorer 5+ or Netscape Navigator 4.7+, Macromedia Flash 5+, Adobe Acrobat Reader 3+

Conventions Used in This Book

In this book, code appears in `monospace` type.

This Book's Organization

The *Design Journal and Course Project Workbook* is divided into 12 chapters:

- Chapter 1, "Foundations of Website Creation," focuses on browsers, HTML, and plug-ins. The lab shows you how to download browsers, utilities, and plug-ins.

- Chapter 2, "Web Page Elements," explores style sheets and multimedia. The lab creates a basic page template for the course project.

- Chapter 3, "Production Tools," compares real-life examples of HTML generating tools. The two labs create a header and logo for the course project.

- Chapter 4, "Pre-Production Process," presents exercises to reinforce the aspects of the pre-production phase including the brainstorming session, surveying competitor sites, and creating mock-ups. The lab in this chapter creates a flowchart and requirements document.

- Chapter 5, "Layout and Design," analyzes how real-life web designers use clarity, consistency, contrast, simplicity, structure, and emphasis in their designs. The labs have you exporting graphics to a web format, creating navigation buttons, and designing a style sheet for the course project.

- Chapter 6, "User Interface Design," focuses on navigation and usability of websites. The labs show you how to add layout items, create navigation items, and set up pages for the course project.

- Chapter 7, "Accessibility and Internationalization," investigates the latest guidelines on making a website accessible for disabled users. In addition, you see how global companies make multiple websites for their international audience. You learn how to perform a simple accessibility test on your website in the lab.

- Chapter 8, "Media Creation," explores optimizing images, creating animations from one or two graphics or text, and analyzing the use of multimedia on websites. The lab in this chapter edits digital images.

- Chapter 9, "Interactivity," focuses on rollover effects, dynamic websites, and the content of forms. The lab sets up a contact form for the course project.

- Chapter 10, "Testing and Optimization," guides you through the process of checking a website for consistency and functionality. The lab creates a home page for the course project.

- Chapter 11, "Implementation and Hosting," explores how cookies, banners, link exchanges, and web rings are used today. The final course project lab shows you how to publish a website.

- Chapter 12, "Portfolio Development," focuses on your portfolio. The lab helps you choose, organize, and prepare materials for a portfolio.

Chapter 1
Foundations of Website Creation

Introduction

Browsers are the programs that display web pages. Before the browser Mosaic was introduced in 1993, only text could be displayed on the web. Now, the most visible function of a browser is its support of media-like images, animations, video, and audio.

Each browser interprets HTML tags differently. So when you design your website, you need to be aware that your pages might not look the same from browser to browser. In this chapter, you compare how the same web pages look in a number of browsers.

URLs combine information about the type of protocol being used, the address of the website where the resource is located, the subdirectory location, and sometimes, the name of the file. It is important for you to know the parts of a URL because you will be naming files and directories. You practice identifying the various parts of URLs in this chapter.

Source code view allows you to see how HTML code looks and how others use HTML code to create certain effects. In this chapter, you study the source code from web pages.

Plug-ins are programs that allow users to play special file formats, such as audio or animation files. Plug-ins are downloaded and installed on users' computers so that they can be automatically accessed by the web browser and displayed inside the browser window to play the desired file. In Lab 1.1, you download browsers and plug-ins. You use these browsers and plug-ins for this course, the course project, and future projects.

Focus Questions

1. What is the role of the W3C?

   _____

   _____

2. What are the three design principles that guide the W3C's activities?

   _____

   _____

3. How did Mosaic change the World Wide Web?

   _____

   _____

4. How do modems work?

_____

_____

5. What is bandwidth?

_____

_____

6. Why is HTML considered universal?

_____

_____

7. What is a domain name?

_____

_____

8. How does a browser work?

_____

_____

9. How does the client/server model of communication work?

_____

_____

10. What is HTTP? What is its most important feature?

_____

_____

Discovery Exercises

URLs

Break down the following URLs to further your understanding of domain names, directories, and filenames.

http://students.netacad.net

Protocol _____

Domain name _____

Directory _____

Filename _____

www.cisco.com

Protocol _____

Domain name _____

Directory _____

Filename _____

www.cisco.com/warp/public/779/edu/academy/stats.html

Protocol _____

Domain name _____

Directory _____

Filename _____

Differences in Browsers

Browsers interpret HTML tags differently. Internet Explorer supports some tags that Netscape Navigator does not (and vice versa). Furthermore, some sites have different versions of their website for each browser (check out www.amazon.com). When designing a website, you need to be aware of how your design will look on different browsers.

1. After you complete Lab 1.1, "Downloading Browsers, Plug-Ins, and Utilities," open Netscape Navigator and Internet Explorer.

   In both browsers, go to www.yahoo.com. Click between the two browsers.

   Does the Yahoo! website look the same on both browsers? If not, what is different?

   _____

   _____

   _____

   _____

2. Go to www.amazon.com on both browsers. Click between them.

   Are there differences? Is the content different?

   _____

   _____

   _____

3. Why would a company like amazon.com create two different websites, one for each browser?

   _____

   _____

   _____

   _____

4. What are some advantages of creating a website for different browsers?

   _____

   _____

   _____

5. What are the disadvantages of creating a website for different browsers?

   _____

   _____

   _____

6. What differences are significant enough between Netscape Navigator and Internet Explorer to affect your web design? (For example, in some instances, Netscape Navigator might not show the outline of boxes while Internet Explorer does).

   _____

   _____

   _____

Text Browsers

7. Check out older browsers at www.evolt.org/browsers. Download Lynx, the text-only browser.

   What is the major difference between the text browsers and graphic browsers, like Internet Explorer and Netscape Navigator?

   _____

   _____

   _____

8. What major features are missing?

   _____

   _____

Source Code View

Go to a search engine like www.altavista.com. If you are using Netscape Navigator, click View, Page Source. If you are using Internet Explorer, click View, Source. Print out the first page of the source code. Keeping the first 10-15 lines of code, trim the page to fit in this space. Paste or tape the code into the following space.

Now go to www.coca-cola.com. Print out the source code for the opening page of this website. Keeping the first 10-15 lines of code, trim the page to fit in the following space. Paste or tape the code into this space.

In Chapter 2 of the curriculum and *Companion Guide*, you learn how to read these source code documents.

Search Engines

Search engines vary in how they search and present information. In this exercise, you use several types of search engines to look for information on the web. An individual engine (www.yahoo.com) uses a spider to collect its own searchable index. A meta engine (www.dogpile.com) searches multiple individual engines simultaneously. Search engines can also be subject-sorted (www.yahoo.com) or relevance-sorted (www.northernlight.com).

Try out these search engines by searching for the same keyword (for example, "North American owls"). Note how the search results differ from one site to another:

- MultiCrawl–www.multicrawl.com
- WebCrawler–www.webcrawler.com
- Alta Vista–www.altavista.com
- Ask Jeeves–www.askjeeves.com
- Google–www.google.com
- LookSmart–www.looksmart.com
- Yahoo!–www.yahoo.com
- Jayde–www.jayde.com/search.html
- HotBot–hotbot.lycos.com
- Lycos–www-english.lycos.com
- Northern Light–www.northernlight.com
- SunSteam–www.sunsteam.com
- WWWomen–www.wwwomen.com

It is a good idea to understand what type of search engine you are using. This also influences your search success. Sort the previous URLs into these categories:

Subject-Sorted Search Engines

_____

_____

_____

Relevance-Sorted Search Engines

_____

_____

_____

Individual Engine

_____

_____

_____

Meta Engine

_____

_____

_____

If you needed to write a paper about North American owls, which five search engines gave you the most appropriate links? Bookmark them for future web searches. (You can also try this exercise with any keyword of your choice.)

My top five search engines:

1. _____

2. _____

3. _____

4. _____

5. _____

Lab 1.1: Downloading Browsers, Plug-Ins, and Utilities

Lab 1.1 describes the locations of and procedures for downloading and installing various essential applications and plug-ins for a typical web workstation. You should reboot your computer after the installation procedure for any of these products is finished, whether you are prompted to do so or not.

Generally speaking, the installation routine for all the following products is the same: Use the link provided to go to the site, select a download button, and when prompted, save the installation file to disk. Save that file where you can easily find it, as you will delete the downloaded file after the installation process is complete. Double-click the file to initiate installation.

Note: When installation is complete, it is always good practice to reboot your computer.

The installation of Internet Explorer is a bit different from other installations. You will be prompted first to download a small (400-500 K) configuration file. After it is downloaded and double-clicked, it contacts an online server where the remainder of the program is downloaded and then installed. The first download is short; the second part is considerably longer.

In any case, whether the installation routine is run online or from a compressed, downloaded installation file, the process will run essentially without further input from the user. When prompted by some programs to verify the storage location of files, it is generally prudent to be agreeable, clicking Yes, OK, Continue, and the like, to accept the default locations and configurations for the programs. If any configurations have to be changed, this can be done after the initial installation by going to a Preferences or Setup menu item.

Toolbox

After downloading the browsers and plug-ins in this chapter, you should save all setup files that you downloaded in a designated toolbox folder on your hard drive (C:). Whenever you download a new utility, use it as the destination and install it from this location.

You should make backup copies of this folder regularly, in case you need to reinstall applications on your computer so you can save time by using your toolbox files.

Another plug-in to download is Adobe's SVG viewer. Download the SVG viewer from www.adobe.com. Save it directly to your toolbox folder. Install the viewer from there.

Internet Explorer

Download the latest or an archived version of Internet Explorer for either the PC or Mac platform from www.microsoft.com/windows/ie/downloads/default.asp

Select the version and platform you want and follow the instructions to download Internet Explorer.

After you launch the Internet Explorer setup file (which will look like "ie5setup.exe"), a dialog box appears and asks you which components you want to install. Check the boxes next to each component and click Enter. After the application finishes installing, it prompts you to restart your computer. When you reboot your machine, Internet Explorer automatically finishes installing itself.

Although you might not want to share personal information (such your name or e-mail address) with the rest of the web, it is sometimes convenient to have easy access to it when, say, you are filling out lots of Internet shopping forms and do not want to repeatedly type this information. On the PC versions, Internet Explorer's My Profile feature conveniently stores your demographic information for such instances. Choose the Tools menu, Internet Options, and select the Content tab. Click the My Profile button under Personal Information, and then either create a new address book entry or select a current one to use for your profile.

The Internet Explorer installation will overwrite any version of Internet Explorer you have previously installed, assuming that you accept all the defaults during the installation process. It will also assume that you want to make it your default browser.

On the PC, if you would like to make another browser the default, you can change this setting in Control Panel, Internet Options, Programs. Uncheck the item that asks if Internet Explorer should check to see whether it is the default browser. Run Netscape and click Yes when asked if you want to make Netscape your default browser.

On the Mac, you can change the default browser under Control Panel, Internet, Web. At the bottom of the pop-up window, a drop-down menu is beside Default Web Browser.

Netscape Navigator

You can download the latest version of Netscape or an older version of Netscape Navigator for either platform (PC or Mac) from home.netscape.com/computing/download.

This link initiates the download without further prompting. The compressed file should be saved to your toolbox folder on your hard drive. Double-clicking the downloaded file begins the installation process, which is typically automatic. Accept all defaults and Netscape will install itself. You might be asked for a name for your initial user profile (simply provide your first initial and last name) before installation is complete. Be sure to reboot when the installation process is complete.

Windows Media Player Plug-In

Note: A typical installation of Internet Explorer PC version 5.5 or later will also install Windows Media Player.

Windows Media Player is available for either platform from www.microsoft.com/windows/windowsmedia/en/download/default.asp.

This link takes you to a screen with a Download button. The compressed file should be saved to your toolbox folder on your hard drive.

Once downloaded, the installation process simply requires a double-click on the installation file (such as mp71.exe). After a warning that all other running applications should be closed before continuing, the installation proceeds without further input (except for clicking OK and Yes buttons). Generally, users should accept all defaults presented during the process.

Flash Player Plug-In

Macromedia Shockwave Player (which includes the Flash download) is available from sdc.shockwave.com/shockwave/download/frameset.fhtml.

No user interaction is required at all once the Download Now button is clicked. The installation is truly automatic, and visual verification is provided on the same screen in the form of a small-screen, interactive Shockwave movie. Upon completion (about 10 minutes on a 56K modem connection), additional Shockwave movie samples are available to show the capabilities of the plug-in.

RealPlayer

RealPlayer Basic is available from www.real.com/player/.

The free Real Player plug-in might be hard to find on the site. The link to the free version is somewhat buried. Look for this link:

RealPlayer 8 Basic - is our free player

You must provide your e-mail address, country of origin, language, operating system, and connection speed.

To install RealPlayer, follow these steps:

1. After the form is filled out, click the Download form button to reveal a new screen.

This screen allows you to make choices among three download options, which are labeled Complete, Standard, and Minimal. The Minimal download will install RealPlayer and the AOL Icon (which you cannot avoid downloading no matter which option you choose), and may be the best choice if you have other choices for playing digital music.

2. After clicking another Download Free RealPlayer Basic Now button, you are prompted to choose a server from which to download the product. After clicking the

link, the following screen appears after several advertisements; click Next to start the installation.

3. An option page appears that asks you how you would like to display the RealPlayer on your computer screen (with shortcuts on your desktop, QuickLaunch tray, etc.). Although all these items are checked by default, you might elect to uncheck all of them with no problem. On the PC, the program always appears in the Programs submenu under Start. On the Mac, the program appears in the Applications folder on your hard drive.

   The last step requires that you submit an electronic registration to Real.com by typing your e-mail address and zip code into another form.

4. You need to choose the speed of your connection. Then you must specify whether you want RealPlayer to be your default player for "supported media types."

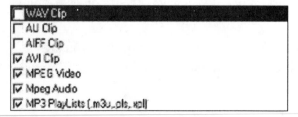

5. Click the Customize button to get a list of the supported media types Real.com is referring to, and uncheck any of the listed formats that other software might already be designated to play.

The next screens bring up channels you can attach to RealPlayer that will help steer you toward the types of information RealPlayer can provide.

You can check any or none of these categories.

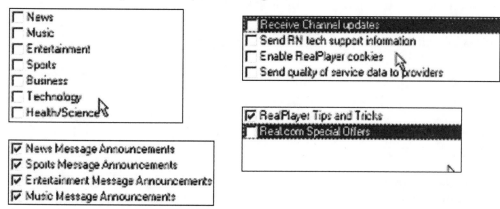

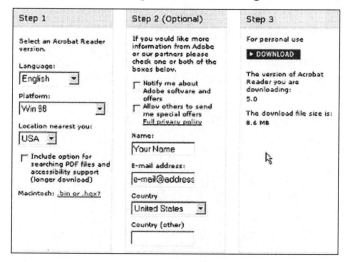

After listing a summary of the options you have chosen, the installation is complete.

Acrobat Reader

Acrobat Reader is available from www.adobe.com/products/acrobat/readstep2.html.

To install Acrobat Reader, follow these steps:

1. Fill out the first two portions of the Registration Form to enable the third step.

2. After clicking the Download button, you are prompted to save the installation file to your toolbox folder.

3. A double-click of the installation file initiates the installation process. After a couple of "agreeable" clicks, the installation is complete.

FTP

Several FTP applications are available for both the PC and the Mac. If you are using a Mac, check out Fetch, the most popular Macintosh FTP program, at fetchsoftworks.com.

In this example, you see how to download and install the PC FTP application WS-FTP LE. It is available from www.ipswitch.com/cgi/download_eval.pl?product=main.

1. Fill out the contact information form on the page to make the download. Note that the radio button next to WS_FTP LE 5.08 is selected.

2. After you fill out the form shown in Step 1, a new page appears, and you are able to download the free product.

All installation steps after the download will proceed much as the others. Again, "agreeable" choices (choices that confirm the reading of any licensing material as well as default placement of files on the local hard drive) will make the process easy.

WinZip and Stuffit

To install WinZip, double-click the downloaded installation file and permit installation of the program. You might be asked to reboot your computer before installation can proceed.

Note: An evaluation version of WinZip is available at www.winzip.com/download.htm. This version is shareware and holds the expectation that you will pay for a copy after a brief evaluation period.

The download link saves the installation file to your toolbox.

A thoughtful feature from the WinZip website provides links to features and frequently asked questions regarding the product.

While the distribution file winzip80.exe is downloading.

- If you haven't ordered yet, you can order online now.
- Browse the Frequently Asked Questions about WinZip.
- Look into the other downloads available from the WinZip web site.
- Check the WinZip Hints and Tips available here on the WinZip web site

Stuffit is a similar compression application that is used by Macintosh and PC users. You can find a free download of the stuffit expander at the following websites:

- www.stuffit.com/expander/macindex.html for Mac users

- www.stuffit.com/expander/winindex.html for PC users

Now you have a toolkit of essential browsers, plug-ins, and utilities on your computer.

Check Your Understanding

1. What are the three concepts that make up the model for web development?

    A. Structure, behavior, interactivity

    B. Presentation, structure, behavior

    C. Presentation, structure, universality

    D. Degradability, universality, behavior

2. Which organization is responsible for assigning IP addresses?

    A. IANA

    B. ISOC

    C. W3C

    D. IETF

3. What organization defines standard Internet operating protocols, such as TCP/IP?

    A. IANA

    B. W3C

    C. IETF

    D. ISDN

4. What is SGML?

    A. A server

    B. The source code for HTML

    C. A protocol

    D. The language that HTML is based on

5. What set of rules allow computers on a network to talk to one another?

    A. Markup language

    B. Protocol

    C. Hypertext

    D. None of the above

6. Which of the following is not one of W3C's goals for the World Wide Web?

    A. Semantic Web

    B. Web of Trust

    C. Incompatibility

    D. Universal access

7. What is the process of translating a computer's binary language into a series of analog waves?

   A. Modulating
   B. Markup
   C. Compiling
   D. None of the above

8. What protocol transfers files created by a web designer to the web server?

   A. TCP
   B. POP3
   C. FTP
   D. ISDN

9. What is the purpose of a search engine?

   A. Provides a peer-to-peer connection
   B. Permits browsing of a network for a specific file
   C. Maintains a database of Internet resources
   D. Enables movement of files from a client to a server

10. Decentralization allows _____ of worldwide proportions.

   A. Evolution
   B. Interoperability
   C. Standardization
   D. Scalability

11. The Internet uses what protocol to exchange information between computers?

   A. TCP/IP
   B. HTTP
   C. FTP
   D. SGML

12. What protocol provides features for addressing?

   A. IP
   B. HTTP
   C. FTP
   D. URL

13. What is the filename in the address http://www.cisco.com/academy/stats.html?

    A. html

    B. stats.html

    C. academy/stats.html

    D. cisco.com/academy/stats.html

14. What is the critical component that Tim Berners-Lee developed that led to the World Wide Web?

    A. A way of giving everything a uniform address

    B. A protocol for transmitting linked bits of information

    C. A language for encoding information

    D. All of the above

15. Which protocol allows a user to save messages in a server mailbox?

    A. SMTP

    B. UDP

    C. POP3

    D. HTTP

16. A server is an application or computer that requests services from a client.

    A. True

    B. False

17. Bandwidth is the physical size of a cable.

    A. True

    B. False

18. Which is a markup language?

    A. HTML

    B. Java

    C. JavaScript

    D. Perl

19. What is the most widely used Internet service?

    A. Gopher

    B. FTP

    C. Instant messenger

    D. E-mail

20. Which organization was originally responsible for the research that led to modern-day networking?

    A. ARPA

    B. ARPNET

    C. NMTP

    D. NCSA

Chapter 2
Web Page Elements

Introduction

Style sheets are files that combine the various style elements to create a personalized look and feel to websites. Instead of hand-coding every web page, you can create a single-coded file that can be referenced. You can have one style sheet or many on your website. In this chapter, you explore the three most common types of style sheets: inline, embedded, and linked.

Demand for more animated features has fueled a surge in the development of multimedia formats. Audio, video, animation, and streaming media are types of multimedia. In this chapter, you will identify the types of multimedia used today in popular websites.

Lab 2.1 helps you create a page template for the course project: the Washington High School website.

Focus Questions

1. What are external style sheets and how can they help web designers?

   _____

   _____

2. What is an example of an element?

   _____

3. What do attributes do?

   _____

4. What is streaming?

   _____

5. Explain the differences between lossy and lossless compression.

   _____

6. What are the advantages of using the GIF format?

   _____

   _____

7. Which type of compression does JPEG use?

   _____

8. Which format would you choose for a simple logo?

   _____

9. Which format would you choose for a photograph that contains many shades, tones, and gradients?

    _____

10. What are the advantages and disadvantages of using PNG?

    _____

    _____

Discovery Exercises

CSS Types

Go online and look for web pages with the three different types of style sheets.

Site 1

Name:_____

URL:_____

CSS Type:_____

How did you recognize this style sheet type? What are the characteristics of this type?

_____

_____

_____

_____

_____

Site 2

Name:_____

CSS Type:_____

How did you recognize this style sheet type? What are the characteristics of this type?

_____

_____

_____

_____

_____

Site 3

Name:_____

URL:_____

CSS Type:_____

How did you recognize this style sheet type? What are the characteristics of this type?

_____

_____

_____

_____

_____

CSS Archive

Browse the web and look for three web pages with designs that you like. If the web pages use style sheets, print out the source code. Copy and paste the source code into your notepad application. Save the source code examples in an Ideas folder for future use. Also, print them and paste the source code on the next few pages for future reference.

Style Sheet 1

URL:_____

Style Sheet 2

URL:_____

Style Sheet 3

URL:_____

Note

If you come across an external style sheet such as this, for example:

```
<link rel="stylesheet" href="global.css">
```

You can access this style sheet by figuring out the path relative to the file that you are viewing.

For example, say that you are viewing www.mysite.com/index.html and, in the source code, the style sheet is linked as <link rel="stylesheet" href="global.css">. You will be able to access or download the style sheet by typing http://www.mysite.com/global.css into the status bar of your browser. By looking at the path pointing to the external style sheet from index.html, you can recognize that the style sheet is in the same directory as the file you are viewing. So, by modifying the URL in your status bar, you will be able to go directly to the CSS file.

Depending on your browser, the reaction might be different. The browser might display the CSS code right away, it might ask you to download the file, or it might even tell you that you do not have access to this file. If you are told you do not have access to this file, try viewing the file in a different browser.

Media Content and Download Times

Browse the web and visit three sites that contain animations, video, or audio clips, such as www.mtv.com, http://movies.warnerbros.com/twister/cmp/trailer.html, www.7up.com, and www.emerils.com. To determine the media type used, right-click an animation or play the video or audio clip. For example, at emerils.com, the logo is a Macromedia Flash animation. The trailer for the movie *Twister* can be viewed either as a .mov or .avi file.

Site 1

Name: _____

URL: _____

Media Type: _____

How did you recognize this style sheet type? What are the characteristics of this type?

_____

_____

_____

_____

_____

What is the file size?_____

How long did it take you to download and view the file?_____

Site 2

Name: _____

URL: _____

Media Type: _____

How did you recognize this style sheet type? What are the characteristics of this type?

_____

_____

_____

_____

_____

What is the file size?_____

How long did it take you to download and view the file?_____

Site 3

Name: _____

URL: _____

Media Type: _____

How did you recognize this style sheet type? What are the characteristics of this type?

_____

_____

_____

_____

_____

What is the file size?_____

How long did it take you to download and view the file?_____

Lab 2.1: Creating the Basic Page Template (GoLive)

In this lab, you create the basic page template for the course project, the Washington High School website. You use Adobe GoLive to create the template. Follow these steps to create the page template:

1. Launch Adobe GoLive 5.0.

2. In the untitled.html page that appears, select the Page Title that reads Welcome to Adobe GoLive 5.

    ▷ 📄 Welcome to Adobe GoLive 5

3. Change the text so that it reads Course Project page template.

    ▷ 📄 Course Project page template

   You will be creating a page template that you will use for all the pages in your course project. This is done to maintain uniformity among the various pages in your website. While you could code this page by hand, this is a great time to practice using Adobe GoLive 5 to accomplish the same goal.

4. Note the Change Window Size indicator in the lower-right corner of your screen. Change it to fit the screen width you will use for your course project. Common screen widths are 640 pixels and 800 pixels. According to most sources, 800 pixels is the most prevalent screen size. However, to accommodate for the lowest common denominator, we changed our Change Windows size indicator to 640 by dragging the lower-right corner of the window until the number 640 appeared.

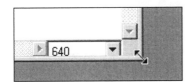

5. Now is a good time to save your page. Because this is a page template, you should save it with a name that indicates its function. Save the file by selecting File, Save As from the menu bar. Save the file in the CourseProject folder with the filename pagetemplate.html.

6. If the Objects palette is not already revealed, select Objects from the Window menu, or you can select Ctrl-2 (PC) or Command-2 (Mac).

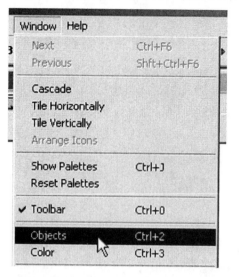

7. In the Objects window, select the Basic tab .

8. Drag the Table icon into the page area.

9. Click a table border until the cursor changes to an arrow with a gray rectangle 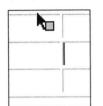.
   At this point, the Table Inspector should appear to the right (in the Palette area). If the Table palette is not showing, select Inspector from the Window menu, or press Ctrl-1 (PC) or Command-1 (Mac).

10. Select the Table tab and change the values in the Table Inspector, as follows:

    a. Rows: 5

    b. Columns: 5

    c. Width: 600 pixel

    d. Border: 0

    e. Cell Pad: 0

    f. Cell Space: 0

11. Deselect the table by clicking the white space around it.

12. Select the top-left cell by moving the cursor slowly over one of the cell's borders until it turns into a white arrow (note that, on the Mac, the arrow stays black), then select the cell by clicking it once.

13. In the Inspector window, with the Cell Tab now in the foreground, change the value in the Column Span field to 5 and press Enter.

Your table will look like this.

You have just created the space for the page header for all pages in the course project.

14. Now create the subheader area by selecting the first cell in the third row by moving the cursor slowly over one of the cell's borders until it turns into a white arrow, then selecting the cell by clicking once on it.

15. Again in the Inspector window with the Cell Tab in front, enter a column span of 5 and press Enter (see Step 13). This creates the subheader area.

16. To create the content and footer areas, apply a column span of 5 to the first cell in the fourth row and the first cell in the fifth row. After deselecting, your table should look like this.

17. To make adding content easier, type the following captions into the table cells.

18. Save your file.

You just created the basic skeleton for a course project page. Based on this template, you can create the home page and all main and subsection pages.

Check Your Understanding

1. In the DOM, a tag is an object and the HTML pages are properties of that object.

   A. True
   B. False

2. What are the two types of images?

   A. Vector and bitmap
   B. Vector and Bezier
   C. Bitmap and GIF
   D. JPEG and WAV

3. The user will see all information contained within which tags?

   A. title
   B. body
   C. html
   D. text

4. The head tag is contained within the title tag.

   A. True
   B. False

5. How many colors or patterns is a GIF image limited to?

   A. 16
   B. 256
   C. 1216
   D. Unlimited

6. What three colors generate color on a computer screen?

   A. Red, yellow, blue
   B. Cyan, magenta, yellow
   C. Red, green, blue
   D. Red, gray, blue

7. _____ consists of a mosaic of individual squares of light.

   A. A vector-based image
   B. A bitmap image
   C. A pixel
   D. Bezier curves

8. What are some interactive elements of a website?

   A. Color, images, animations
   B. HTML forms, e-mail, Java applets
   C. HTML forms, animations, e-mail
   D. HTML forms, JavaScripts, images

9. Which tag provides keyword information about the content of that page to search engines?

   A. body
   B. head
   C. meta
   D. title

10. Which tag and attribute are used to create a hyperlink?

    A. <link>
    B. <link href>
    C. <a href>
    D. <anchor link>

11. The image tag allows you to add attributes that control the action and appearance of an image.

    A. True
    B. False

12. Which image format has ownership restrictions for the use of the compression technology?

    A. PNG
    B. GIF
    C. BMP
    D. JPEG

13. What kind of link is <a href="mypage.htm">mypage</a>?

    A. Absolute
    B. Dynamic
    C. Relative
    D. Frameset

14. What attribute in the image tag is required to direct the HTML to get the image?

    A. href=
    B. src=
    C. get=
    D. none of the above

15. What can be used to control the layout and positioning of web page elements?

    A. Tables and links
    B. Tables and frames
    C. Frames and lists
    D. Links and frames

16. How is color delivered to a computer screen?

    A. The computer generates light.
    B. The computer absorbs light.

17. Which format would be chosen when creating an image to be put on a web page?

    A. JPEG
    B. AIFF
    C. PSD
    D. WAV

18. Lossy is the compression scheme to use if you want a small file size and are willing to sacrifice the original quality of the image.

    A. True
    B. False

19. Which audio type takes the least amount of storage on a disk?

    A. AVI
    B. AIFF
    C. MP3
    D. WAV

20. Which of the following will display the guitar.gif file on the web page if the file is located in the images folder, which is in the same directory as the HTML document?

    A. <img src="images/guitar.gif">
    B. <img src="guitar.gif">
    C. <img src="C:/projects/images/guitar.gif">
    D. <img src="projects/images/guitar.gif">

Chapter 3
Production Tools

Introduction

You can generate HTML in two primary ways—doing it by hand in a text editor, or using a What-You-See-Is-What-You-Get (WYSIWYG) editor. Professional web designers often find that they must be able to do both to have the most control over their documents and designs.

In this chapter, you generate small HTML documents using text editors, word processors, and spreadsheet applications. Then you compare the code generated in those applications with the code generated in WYSIWYG editors, such as Adobe GoLive.

The two labs in this chapter help you create the header and logo for the Washington High School website course project. You use Adobe Photoshop to create the header and Adobe Illustrator to create the logo.

Focus Questions

1. Why are templates useful?

   _____

   _____

2. What are the advantages of using an HTML conversion utility?

   _____

   _____

3. What produces fat code?

   _____

   _____

4. Which method usually produces the cleanest code?

   _____

   _____

5. What are some of the common features of HTML editors?

   _____

   _____

6. What is the difference between bitmap and vector applications?

   _____

   _____

7. Which applications would you use to create interactive navigation such as rollovers?

_____

_____

8. Which type of graphics program would you choose if you wanted to edit a photograph?

_____

9. What is the major disadvantage of using WYSIWYG editors?

_____

_____

10. Which applications can create SWF files?

_____

_____

Discovery Exercises

Open a WYSIWYG editor such as Adobe GoLive or Microsoft FrontPage. You now explore the web capabilities of this application. Create a web page by adding the following table to a simple layout.

State	Capital	State Flower
Arizona	Phoenix	
California	Sacramento	
Illinois	Springfield	
Colorado	Denver	

Save this page as an HTML file.

1. View the page in your browser and look at the source code. On the following lines, note which parts of the code are repetitive or unnecessary (for example, certain tags).

_____

_____

_____

_____

Now open Microsoft Word or another word-processing application. Create a web page by the previous table. Save this page as an HTML file.

2. View the page in your browser and look at the source code. On the following lines, note which parts of the code are repetitive or unnecessary (for example, certain tags).

_____

_____

_____

_____

3. Open Microsoft Excel or another spreadsheet application and create a simple spreadsheet using the previous table. Save it as HTML. Open it in your browser and view the source code. On the following lines, note which parts of the code are repetitive or unnecessary (for example, certain tags).

_____

_____

_____

_____

4. What is the difference between the code generated by one of these applications and code that you type or create by using an HTML editor?

    _____

    _____

    _____

    _____

5. Which alternative produces the "leanest" and which the "fattest" code?

    By WYSIWYG Editor (for example, Adobe GoLive): _____

    By Office Application (for example, Microsoft Word): _____

Lab 3.1: Creating the Header in Adobe Photoshop

In this lab, you learn to create a title header for your future web pages.

You use the text tools and colors to make your title header unique to your website.

1. Open Adobe Photoshop. Set your ruler units to pixels by selecting Edit, Preferences, Units & Rulers from the menu bar. Use the drop-down menu to select pixels for Rulers. Click OK. (It is important that you set the unit of measurement to pixels when designing for the web. Other units of measurement, such as inches, centimeters, and percentage, are used for different types of media.)

2. Create a new file by selecting File, New. The New dialog box appears.

3. In the New dialog box, name your new file header, and type in the corresponding image size of width 600 pixels, height 110 pixels, and resolution 72 pixels/inch. Mode should be RGB Color, and the Contents should be White. Click OK.

Now that the new file has been created, it is time to set your color palette. Because you already know that your title header will be placed on a web page, it is important to create your header using web-safe colors. By using web-safe colors, you are assured that what you create will be the same when it is viewed over the Internet.

4. To select a web-safe palette in Photoshop, choose Window, Show Swatches.

5. Click the palette menu, which is the small black triangle in the upper-right corner of the color palette box. You are now able to select from a large selection of swatch palettes. Click the selection named Web Safe Colors.aco, as shown in the accompanying figure.

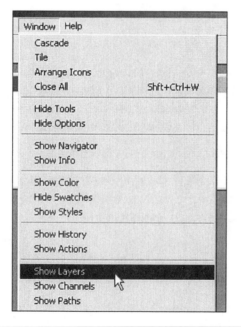

6. Click OK when prompted to replace the current color swatch with the Web Safe Colors.aco.

7. Whenever you work in Photoshop, be sure to have your layer palette open and viewable. Open the Layers palette by selecting Window, Show Layers from the menu bar.

8. The Layers palette appears.

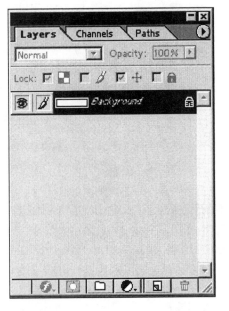

9. In the toolbox, select the Type tool .

10. Click in the white space of your header.psd window and note how the tool options bar for the Type tool appears right beneath the menu bar.

11. Type the word Washington in the white space and make sure the Left Align text option 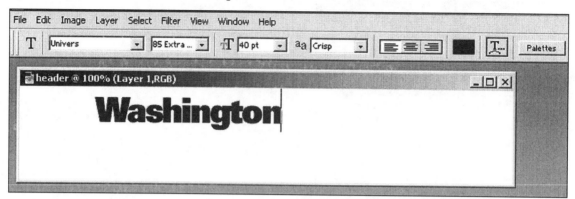 is selected in the tool options bar.

12. To format your text correctly, select the word Washington by highlighting it. Set the font family to Univers (a), the font style to 85 Extra Black (b), the font size to 50 pt and font anti-aliasing method to Crisp (c). If these font options are not available to you, choose another sans serif font. Finally, set the text color by clicking the font Color Indicator (d). When the Color Picker window opens, select the web-safe color RGB 51, 102, 153; the hexadecimal representation of this color is #336699 (e).

a)

b)

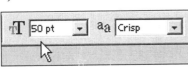

| 39 Thin Ultra Condensed |
| 59 Ultra Condensed |
| 47 Condensed Light |
| 47 Condensed Light Oblique |
| 57 Condensed |
| 57 Condensed Oblique |
| 67 Condensed Bold |
| 67 Condensed Bold Oblique |
| 45 Light |
| 45 Light Oblique |
| 55 Roman |
| 55 Oblique |
| 65 Bold |
| 65 Bold Oblique |
| 75 Black |
| 85 Extra Black |
| 75 Black Oblique |
| 85 Extra Black Oblique |

c)

d)

e)

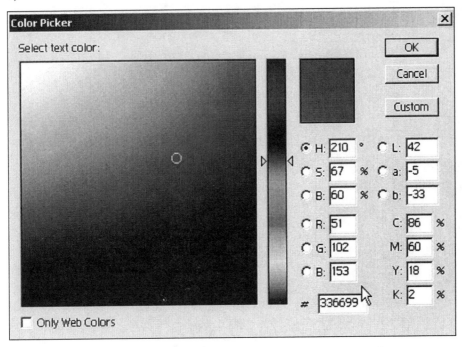

Click OK to close the Color Picker dialog box.

13. Now the tracking (horizontal white space between the letters) needs to be adjusted. First, you need to open the Character palette by selecting Window, Show Character from the menu bar.

14. In the Character window, enter a tracking of 25.

15. Click the checkmark icon on the right side of the tool options bar to commit the changes made with the Type tool. Save your file in a folder called layout under the name header.psd.

16. Select the Type tool again, and type the words High School in the white space of your header.psd.

17. Highlight the words High School. Make the following selections in the tool options bar: Sabon, Roman, 24 pt, crisp, RGB: 51,102,153. If these font options are not available to you, choose another serif font. On the Character palette, set the tracking for these words to 5.

18. Now you need to move the text layers. (Look at your Layers palette; there are now two additional Type Layers.) Select View, Show Rulers to display the rulers.

View	Window	Help	
New View			
Proof Setup		▶	
Proof Colors		Ctrl+Y	
Gamut Warning		Shft+Ctrl+Y	
Zoom In		Ctrl++	
Zoom Out		Ctrl+-	
Fit on Screen		Ctrl+0	
Actual Pixels		Alt+Ctrl+0	
Print Size			
✔ Show Extras		Ctrl+H	
Show		▶	
Show Rulers		Ctrl+R	
✔ Snap		Ctrl+;	

19. .Now create a vertical guide to help you position your text by left-clicking and dragging the mouse starting from the left ruler and align it with the 11-pixel marker on the top ruler. Release the mouse button to create the guide. You might need to zoom in to 200% to better view the selection. (Use the Zoom tool or the box located in the lower-left corner.)

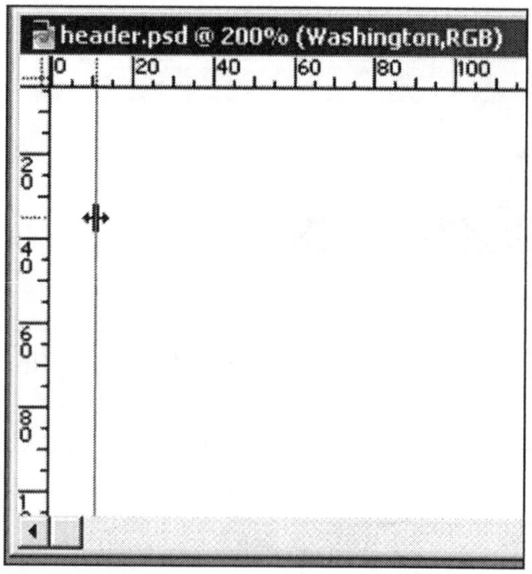

20. Now create the horizontal guide by dragging the mouse starting from the top ruler and aligning it with the 65-pixel marker on the left ruler. If you need to adjust your guide, select the Move tool from the toolbox and then make the adjustment. Select View, Snap To and make sure there is a checkmark next to the Guides option. This helps you line up the text with the guides.

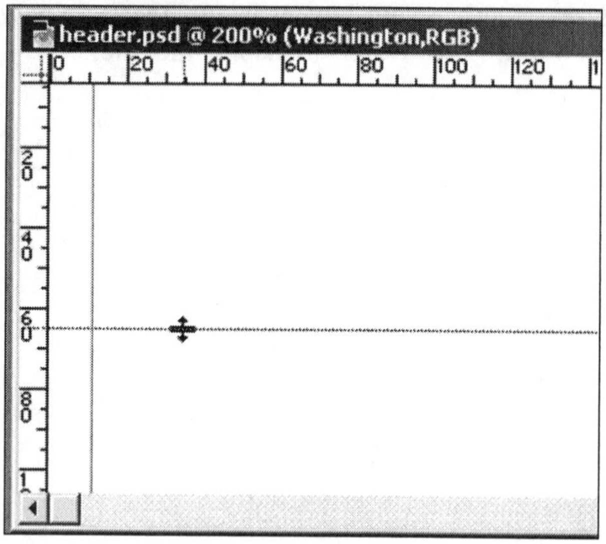

21. You can move the Washington layer by choosing the Move tool  from the toolbox. Select the Washington layer in your Layers palette. Drag the word Washington so that the left and bottom borders of the W are aligned with the guides, as shown here.

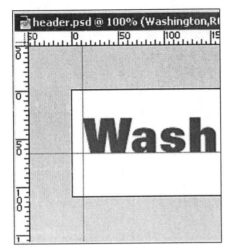

22. Save your file in the Course Project folder.

23. Now create another pair of guides at 248 pixels horizontal (X) and 92 pixels vertical (Y).

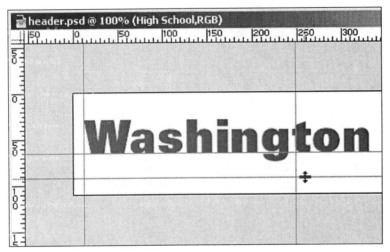

24. Select the High School layer in the Layer palette. Now you can move the High School so that the left and bottom borders of the "H" are aligned with the guides.

25. Save your file.

Lab 3.2: Creating a Logo in Adobe Illustrator

In this lab, you learn to use Adobe Illustrator to create a vector-based design logo.

You will complete the lizard logo and export it to use in your header.psd. If you desire, you can also create the complete lizard on your own, using the template to help you.

1. Start Illustrator. Open the lizard.ai file via the File, Open menu item. This file contains two lizard images.

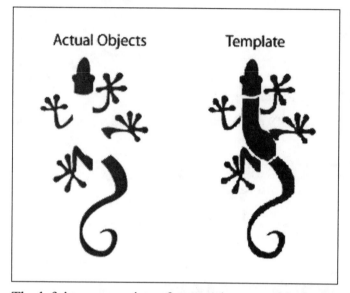

The left image consists of grouped vector objects that will make up the final logo, after the missing object for the body has been created. The right image is a bitmap that has been placed into this Illustrator file to serve as a template and to help you create the body object.

2. To be able to retrace the body object of the lizard exactly, it is necessary to move the template so that it is directly beneath the actual objects. To achieve this, you could click the template and drag it manually. This method, however, can be a bit inaccurate. Therefore, it is a good idea to take advantage of the Align Palette feature that Illustrator offers. Open the Align Palette by clicking Window, Show Align.

Window	Help	
New Window		
Cascade		
Tile		
Arrange Icons		
Hide Tools		
Show Appearance	Shift+F6	
Show Navigator		
Show Info	F8	
Show Color	F6	
Show Attributes	F11	
Show Transparency	Shift+F10	
Show Stroke	F10	
Show Gradient	F9	
Show Styles	Shift+F5	
Style Libraries	▶	
Show Brushes	F5	
Brush Libraries	▶	
Show Swatches		
Swatch Libraries	▶	
Show Layers	F7	
Show Actions		
Show Links		
Show SVG Interactivity		
Show Transform	Shift+F8	
Show Align	Shift+F7	
Show Pathfinder	Shift+F9	

3. Now select the template and the actual objects group by clicking the template while holding down the Shift key and clicking on the actual objects group. You should now have both objects selected, as shown here.

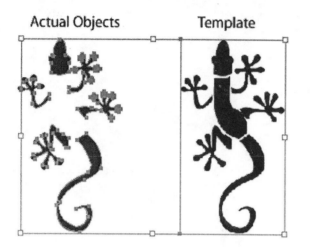

4. Then you can align them with the help of the Align Palette by first clicking the Horizontal Align Center button.

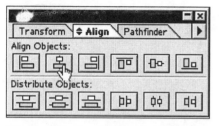

5. Now click the Vertical Align Center button.

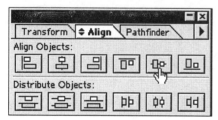

The result should look like this.

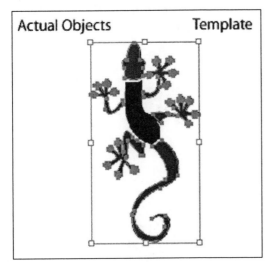

6. Now deselect the objects by clicking the surrounding white space.

7. Select File, Save As to save your file to the Course Project folder. Click OK when prompted by the Illustrator Native Format Options window.

8. Before you start drawing the body, you need to set the stroke and fill color to another color, so you can see what you are drawing against the black template. On your toolbar, click the fill color area to open up the color palette.

The color palette opens up.

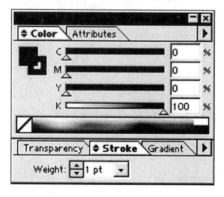

9. Set the color mode to RGB by clicking the black arrow in the top-right corner of the Color Palette and selecting RGB.

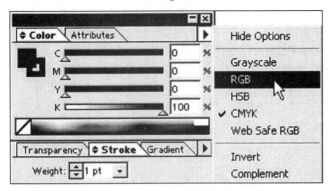

10. In RGB mode, set the fill color to red (RGB: 255,0,0) and press Enter.

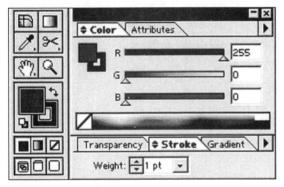

11. Now click the Stroke Color area to set the stroke color, either on your toolbar or Color Palette.

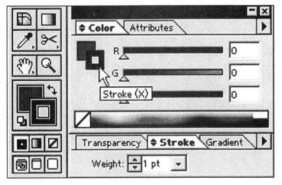

12. Enter the same RGB value, R=255, as the fill color and press Enter.

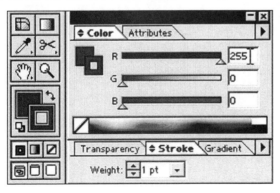

13. Save your file.

14. Now select the Zoom Tool  and zoom in on the body area.

15. Select the Pencil Tool 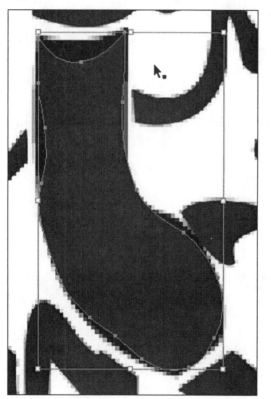 and trace the outline of the lizard's body in one stroke until you reach the starting point (to close the path), then let go. A new body object appears.

16. To add to the object, use the Selection tool to select it (so it shows the blue box around it). With the Pencil tool, draw the area you want to add, starting and ending at the object's border (a). The mouse is represented by a Pencil tool when you release the mouse after adding to the object. (b) You might need to zoom in a bit more.

a)

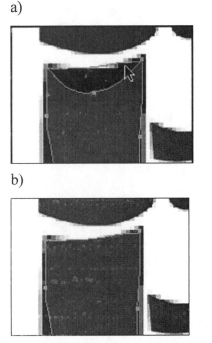

b)

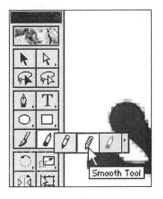

17. Continue by adding areas to your object until it covers the complete template's body.

18. In case you draw a line that does not work, select Edit, Undo Pencil from the menu bar or use the keys Ctrl-Z (PC) or Command-Z (Mac) to undo this step.

19. Hold the left mouse button down on the Pencil tool until the hidden tools appear. Select the Smooth tool to smooth out the edges.

20. After that, you can use the Erase tool 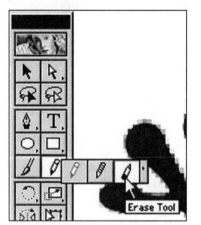 to erase over standing edges of your object, if necessary. Be careful not to destroy the object; use the Undo function (or keys) if you make a mistake.

21. Save your file.

22. Now that you have completed the lizard, you can zoom out. Using the drop-down menu in the lower-left hand corner of the Illustrator window, select Fit On Screen.

6400%
4800%
3200%
2400%
1600%
1200%
800%
600%
400%
300%
200%
150%
100%
66.67%
50%
33.33%
25%
16.67%
12.5%
8.33%
6.25%
4.17%
3.13%

Fit On Screen
53.89%

23. To prepare the vector lizard for exporting, you need to remove the template lizard. To do this, click the white space in the proximity of the lizard shapes until a blue selection box appears. If you select the actual objects lizard, use Shift-Click to add the body you just drew to the selection. Then use the arrow keys to move the selected object to the left. If you select the template, it looks like this.

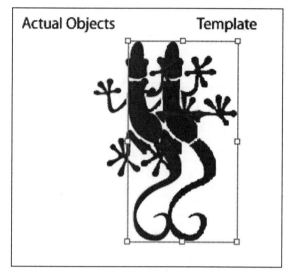

24. Move the template to the far right side of your page so that you can easily select the actual objects and the lizard's body object. Select them together by holding down the Shift key.

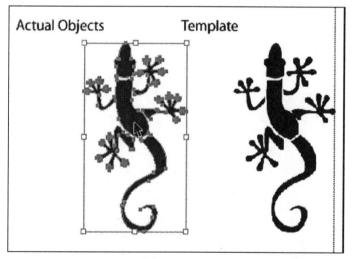

25. Now ungroup these objects by selecting the Object, Ungroup menu item.

26. With the objects still selected, change the fill and stroke color to black (RGB: 0,0,0) by using the Color Palette.

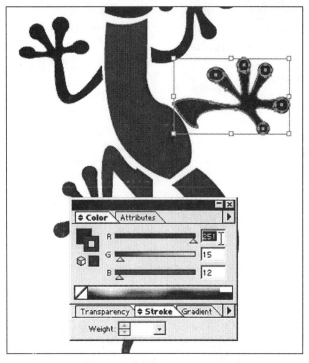

27. Now group the lizard objects together. By doing this, you can export them without losing the arrangement. First, select all objects with the help of the Shift key (make sure to get them all, if they are not all still selected), then select the Object, Group menu item.

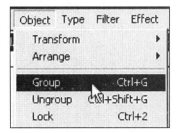

28. Save your file as lizard.ai.

29. Export your file as lizard.psd to the Course Project folder via the File, Export menu item.

Make sure that these options are switched on when the Photoshop Options window appears.

30. Start Photoshop and open lizard.psd.

31. After lizard.psd is open, select the image of the actual vector lizard on the left (not the template on the right) with the Rectangular Marquee tool 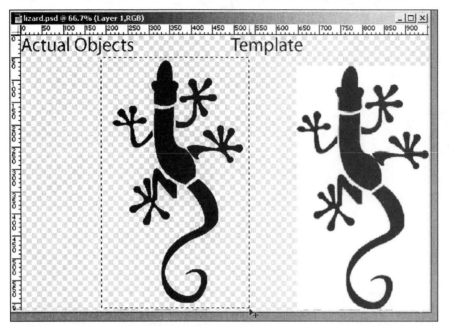.

32. Press the Ctrl-C keys (PC) or Command-C keys (Mac) to copy the contents of the selected area, and press the Ctrl-V keys (PC) or Command-C keys (Mac) to paste the contents of the selection as a layer. (*Note*: In the following figure, the marquee icon, which is the small box with moving edges placed over the hand icon, would only be present if you pressed the Option key while selecting the layer. Normally, you just see the hand icon. You do not need the marquee icon for this step.)

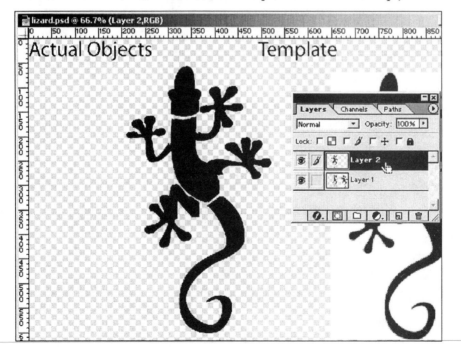

33. Now duplicate layer 2 by clicking the black arrow of the palette menu on the top-left corner of the Layers window and selecting Duplicate Layer.

You now have three layers in your Layers window.

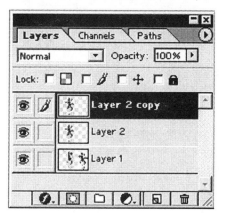

34. To make image editing easier, hide the two bottom layers by clicking the eye icons in the Layers palette and make sure the Layer 2 Copy layer is selected.

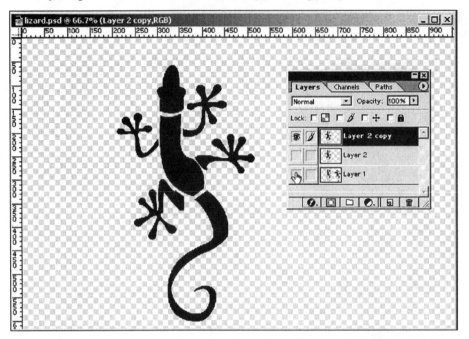

35. Rotate the visible top layer by selecting the Edit, Transform, 90 CCW menu item; this rotates the layer by 90 degrees counter-clockwise.

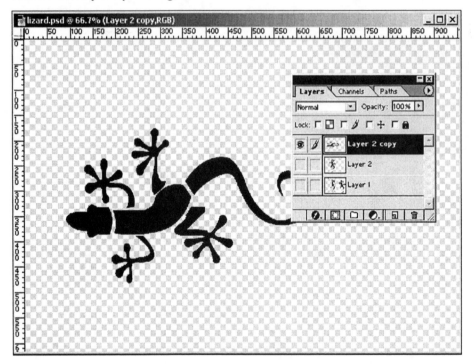

36. You need to scale the layer by selecting the Edit, Transform, Scale menu item.

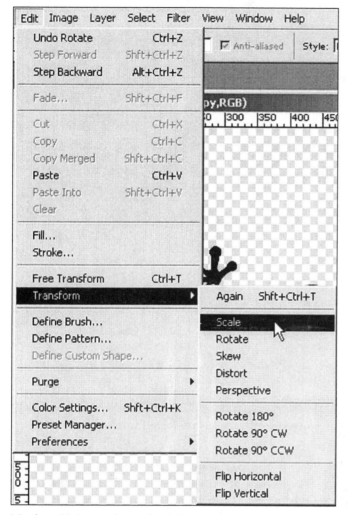

Notice that a scale options bar appears beneath the menu items on the top of the Photoshop window.

37. To change a layer size in pixels, you need to enter the pixel number in the width (W) or height (H) option boxes. To keep the proportions of the layer when changing the size, click the chain icon ⌷ between W and H in the width text box (W), type in 130px, and click the checkmark icon to commit the changes.

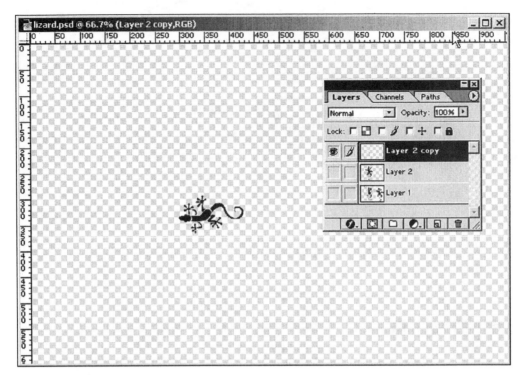

38. Save your file.

39. Hide the top layer and show the middle layer by clicking on the respective eye icon.

40. Select the middle layer to edit it by clicking Layer 2 in the Layers palette.

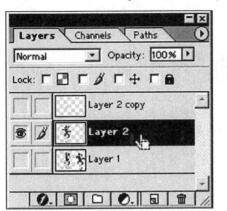

41. Rotate this layer 90 degrees counter-clockwise as you did before, then scale this layer to 55% (remember to click the Chain icon), and commit the changes.

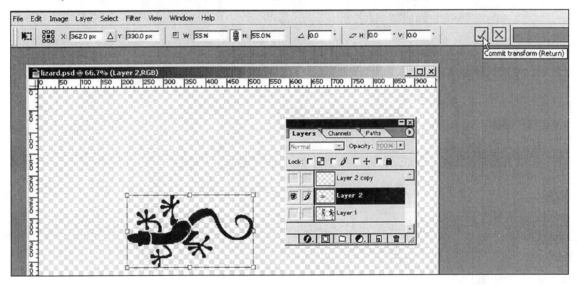

42. This layer needs to be rotated by a manual amount. Go to Edit, Transform, Rotate.

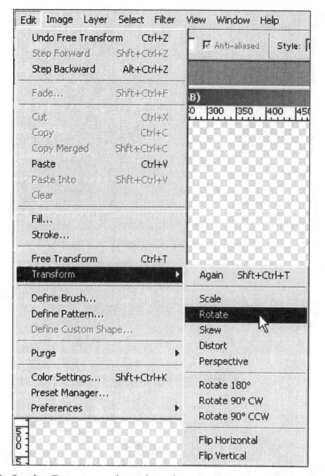

43. In the Rotate options bar that appears beneath the menu, enter -6.5 in the Set Rotation options box. After that, commit the changes by clicking the checkmark.

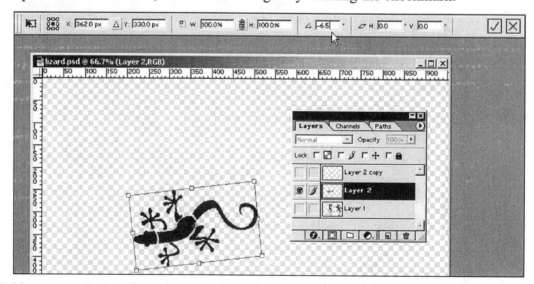

44. Now open the header.psd that is already in your layout folder.

45. Create new guides to place the small lizard correctly in the header area: vertical guide at the 456 marker and the horizontal guide at the 97 marker.

46. Switch back to lizard.psd now by selecting the Window menu item and choosing the lizard.psd option at the bottom.

Window | Help
- Cascade
- Tile
- Arrange Icons
- Close All   Shft+Ctrl+W
- Hide Tools
- Hide Options
- Show Navigator
- Hide Info
- Show Color
- Show Swatches
- Show Styles
- Show History
- Show Actions
- Hide Layers
- Show Channels
- Show Paths
- Hide Character
- Show Paragraph
- Hide Status Bar
- Reset Palette Locations
- ✔ 1 header.psd @ 200% (Layer 2,RGB)
- 2 lizard.psd @ 66.7% (Layer 2,RGB)

47. In lizard.psd, activate the top layer by clicking it in the Layers palette. (*Note:* In the following figure, the marquee icon, which is the small box with moving edges placed over the Hand icon, would only be present if you pressed the Option key while selecting the layer. Normally, you just see the Hand icon. You do not need the marquee icon for this step.)

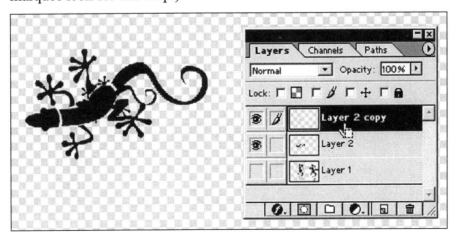

48. Press the keys Ctrl-A (PC) or Command-A (Mac) to select all objects on the active layer, and press Ctrl-C (PC) or Command-A (Mac) to copy all selected objects to the cache.

49. To create a new layer in the header.psd, go back to the header.psd (using the Window menu item like you did before), and press Ctrl-V (PC) or Command-V (Mac) to paste the small lizard that you just copied from the lizard.psd as a layer to the header.psd. Alternatively, use the Move tool from the toolbox to drag the lizard onto the header.psd file.

50. With the Move tool still selected , move the small lizard by dragging him so that the left and bottom borders of the animal are aligned with the guides that you created before (paying attention not to confuse the guides).

51. Create new guides to place the large lizard correctly in the header area: vertical guide at the 382 marker and horizontal guide at the 87 marker; zoom in, if necessary.

52. Save the header.psd by pressing Ctrl-S (PC) or Command-S (Mac).

53. Go back to lizard.psd.

54. In lizard.psd, hide the top layer showing the small lizard (a) and activate the middle layer showing the large lizard on the Layers palette (b).

a)

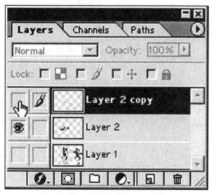

b)

55. Use Ctrl-A (PC) or Command-A (Mac) to select all objects on the active layer and use Ctrl-C (PC) or Command-C (Mac) to copy all selected objects to the cache.

56. Use the Move tool to drag the large lizard onto header.psd.

57. Reposition the large lizard layer with the Move tool ⌖. Drag it so that the left guide aligns with the lizard's nose and the bottom guide aligns with its bottom eye (make sure not to confuse the guides).

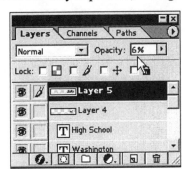

58. In the Layer palette, change the opacity of the large lizard (the active layer) to 6%.

59. In the Layers window, drag the top layer (large lizard) down by one (a) so that it is in the background of the small lizard (b).

a)

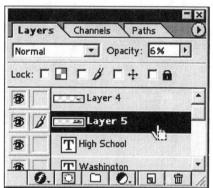

b)

60. You have now created the complete header consisting of the two text layers and the two lizard layers. In addition, you have successfully positioned them so that your file looks like this.

61. Save your header.psd and lizard.psd files.

Check Your Understanding

1. Which approach to coding gives you the most control over HTML code?

    A. Using text editors
    B. Using HTML editors
    C. Using HTML conversion utilities
    D. Using WYSIWYG editors

2. What are the advantages of HTML editors?

    A. Browser-like preview of completed page
    B. Comprehensive site maintenance
    C. Tools such as spell-checking and tag interfaces
    D. Integrated with photo editors

3. Which of the following is a benefit of using templates for HTML documents?

    A. Increase speed
    B. Ensure accuracy
    C. Maintain consistency
    D. All of the above

4. What are the most popular vector-based graphic applications?

    A. Adobe Photoshop, Macromedia Fireworks, Corel PhotoPaint
    B. Adobe Photoshop, Macromedia Freehand, Corel Draw
    C. Adobe Illustrator, Macromedia Fireworks, Corel PhotoPaint
    D. Adobe Illustrator, Macromedia Freehand, Corel Draw

5. In what format will a tool used to create animated vector graphics for the web most likely export files?

    A. GIF
    B. PNG
    C. SWF
    D. VEC

6. Which application is used to edit bitmap images?

    A. Corel Draw
    B. Adobe Illustrator
    C. Macromedia Freehand
    D. Adobe Photoshop

7. What type of application is Adobe LiveMotion?

    A. WYSIWYG editor
    B. HTML editor
    C. Animation
    D. Video

8. The number of pixels determines the quality of a vector graphic.

    A. True
    B. False

9. What is the term used to describe code filled with unnecessary tags?

    A. Padded
    B. Markup
    C. Fat
    D. WYSIWYG

10. WYSIWYG editors support CSS.

    A. True
    B. False

11. When hard-coding a page, which order would the HTML tags be used?

    A. <head></head><title></title><body></body>
    B. <head><title></title></head><body></body>
    C. <title><head></head></title><body></body>
    D. <head><title><body></body></title></head>

12. Which approach to coding gives you the least control over HTML code?

    A. Hand-coding
    B. Using WYSIWYG editors
    C. Using HTML conversion utilities
    D. Both B and C

13. What can be incorporated into an SWF file?

    A. Video
    B. Audio
    C. Animation
    D. Both B and C

14. Which type of application uses Bezier curves?

    A. Bitmap graphic

    B. Vector graphic

    C. Both

    D. None on the above

15. Which application would you choose to manipulate photographs for your website?

    A. Adobe Illustrator or Macromedia Freehand

    B. Adobe Photoshop or Adobe Illustrator

    C. Adobe Photoshop or Macromedia Fireworks

    D. Adobe GoLive or Microsoft FrontPage

16. Text editors such as Notepad and SimpleText are native or freely available within most operating systems.

    A. True

    B. False

17. Which type of application speeds up coding but produces fat code?

    A. WYSIWYG editor

    B. HTML conversion utility

    C. Text editor

    D. All of the above

18. Which type of format creates small and scalable animations?

    A. Animated GIF

    B. Flash

    C. QuickTime

    D. None of the above

19. What features do audio and video tools, such as Adobe Premiere and Apple QuickTime, offer web designers?

    A. The ability to edit audio and video clips

    B. Video filters

    C. Export to web formats

    D. All of the above

20. Which of the following formats allow(s) you to create streaming multimedia?

    A. RealProducer and Windows Media

    B. Animated GIFs

    C. Dynamic HTML

    D. Adobe GoLive and Adobe LiveMotion

Chapter 4
Pre-Production Process

Introduction

The pre-production phase of the web design process involves gathering information from the client, determining the goal of the website, surveying competitors' sites, and presenting the client with mock-ups of the website. In this chapter, you conduct a competition survey and create mock-ups for the website of an established company.

Also in this chapter, you create a flowchart for the course project.

Focus Questions

1. What is the purpose of the brainstorming session?

   _____

   _____

2. What are some of the best ways to back up files and assets?

   _____

   _____

3. What should be considered when determining the scope of a site?

   _____

   _____

4. What should be the main goal of your work on your client's website?

   _____

   _____

5. What is information architecture?

   _____

   _____

6. What is contained in a requirements document?

   _____

   _____

7. What does a web master do?

   _____

   _____

8. What should you do before meeting with a client for the first time?

_____

_____

9. What kind of assets will you need from the client?

_____

_____

10. What is the naming convention for the home page?

_____

_____

Discovery Exercises

Competition Survey

You are designing a website for an online bookstore. You need to conduct a survey of the client's competition. Find three online bookstores or go to www.amazon.com, www.bn.com, and www.borders.com.

1. What do all these sites have in common?

    _____

    _____

    _____

    _____

    _____

2. What are some unique features of each?

    Site 1: _____

    Site 2: _____

    Site 3: _____

3. Which features would you incorporate into an online bookstore?

    _____

    _____

    _____

    _____

    _____

Mock-Ups

Think about how companies use design. Are there companies that immediately come to mind? Coca-Cola, McDonalds, and Nike are just some of the companies whose use of design is so successful that we associate colors or symbols with them. What would happen if Coca-Cola switched colors from red and white to blue and white? Would we instantly recognize a coke can or advertisement? Probably not. The same is true for the golden arches of McDonalds or Nike's swoosh.

Although it is important for companies to maintain the key components of their designs which are recognizable, they continually update their designs. Coca-Cola, for example, is continually revising its packaging and advertising designs. To determine the new look, companies prepare several design possibilities, called *mock-ups*.

Select a product or company (choose your own or use Coca-Cola) and create two new designs, mock-ups, for the home page of a website that incorporates the important elements of that company such as color, logos, and other visual elements. You can either make a sketch of your mock-ups in this workbook or use Adobe Photoshop or Adobe Illustrator to create digital mock-ups.

First Mock-Up

Company name: _____

Second Mock-Up

Company name: _____

Lab 4.1: Creating a Flowchart

Part I: Formulating the Outline

One of the first things to consider when getting ready to assemble a requirements document is how the various parts will fit together. That is, a cohesive, organized structure must be laid in place before the requirements document can be realized and drawn up. One of the best ways to ensure that the project will be organized from the first step is to build an outline.

There are five basic steps in building such an outline:

1. Make a wish list. During the concept stage, when you do your initial planning with your client(s) and your partner(s), jot down a wish list of all the content that the site will include. This gives you an idea of the size and scope of the project.

   In this lab, you use the course project to create a flowchart.

   During the brainstorming session for the Washington High School website, the following ideas were gathered:

   - Place for information regarding upcoming athletic events
   - Latest news stories
   - A way to communicate with teachers
   - Alumni—reunions
   - Alumni list

   - Special programs in the curriculum
   - Calendar of school events
   - Important old news stories
   - A form for users to contact web designers
   - Classes offered at Washington High

2. Organize the content into groups. From the wish list, you can begin to organize the content into logical groups. For example, from the wish list we might be able to discern specific groups of content: information, activities, programs, and contact. Organize the wish list into categories for the Washington High School website.

3. Create categories from the groups. After you have a few groups of content, you will begin to see a pattern emerging. Some groups are similar so you can lump them together into larger categories. Other groups might need to be more clearly defined so they may be split apart. The key to developing a successful site plan is precision. Try to identify the smallest number of distinct categories that will still meet your client's needs. For the Washington High School website, five specific categories exist: News, Calendar, Curriculum, Alumni, and Contacts.

Compare your categorization with the following categories and subcategories:

- News
  - Current
  - Archived
- Calendar
  - School
  - Athletic

- Curriculum
  - Programs
  - Special programs
- Alumni
  - News
  - List

- Contacts
  - Teacher list
  - Contact form

4. Build the outline. As you can see in Step 3, the outline practically builds itself. The categories become the main ideas. Below the categories are any subcategories, and within those subcategories are lists of content. Generally, the lists of content are the pages that will require the most regular updating.

5. Make a quick sketch of the site flowchart. Based on the outline you have conceived, create a flowchart of the website. You can create it in a word-processing or spreadsheet program or even sketch it on paper. Though you might revise the site flowchart later in the pre-production process (see Part II of this lab), the visual prediction of the site's structure is a handy guide to follow as you develop the requirements document.

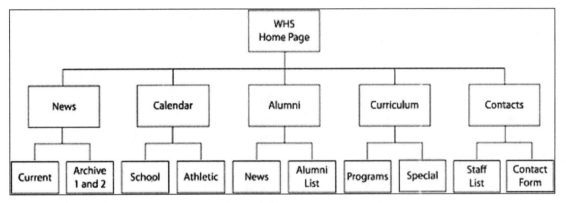

Part II: Formulating the Requirements Document

The flowchart you created in Part I lays out the proposed site in big chunks. The requirements document, which you formulate in this part of the lab, breaks those chunks into their component pieces.

Before compiling the requirements document for the Washington High School website, the answers to these questions should be determined:

- Who will be the Washington High School contacts to provide updated information to the web designer?

- For each of the categories established in the outline, how often will the high school expect information to be updated?

- What kinds of resources (hardware and software) must the school provide to make sure the updating can be done on a regular basis?

- What are the daily/weekly/monthly/bi-yearly tasks the web designer needs to accomplish?

After these questions are considered and answers are delivered, a more formal list of tasks, assets, and requirements that are required to construct the site can be laid out. You can create a table similar to Table 4-1 to list essential site requirements:

Table 4-1: Requirements Document

Job	Materials	Details	Assigned to/ Update Schedule
Note: All updating of the Washington High School website is to be accomplished in the Media Room. A computer with 24/7 Internet access has been set aside to accomplish the updating. The computer is under the supervision of Mr. X, the media teacher, and will be manned by the website team.			

• Layout of site, beginning with functional mock-up	• Apply school colors to mock-up.
	• Include school logo.
	• Create new navigation scheme with five color schemes and icons.
		• Make sure color scheme is web-safe.
		• Plan navigation three ways.
		  - Navigation bar
		  - Econ
		  - Text equivalent
			• Design team/updated yearly

• Create school logo graphic.	• Use Adobe Illustrator for creation. • Convert to GIF.	• Design to run alongside WHS headline on all pages.	• Design team
• Decide on school color-compliant color scheme.	• Create color palette in Photoshop.	• Color scheme will remain consistent over all pages.	• Design team
• Create five icons to correspond to five agreed-on categories in initial outline.	• Use Photoshop and ImageReady to create mouseover and mouseout states.	• Create GIFs for mouseover and mouseout button states for icons (icon + Alt tags).	• Design team
• Create navigation bar to correspond to icons above.		• Create GIFs for mouseover and mouseout button states for navigation (navigation + Alt tags) bar.	• Design team

Job	Materials	Details	Assigned to/ Update Schedule

• Style guide
 	
  - Icon logo
  - School colors
  - Color scheme
  - Typefaces
	• Style guide elements (will be joined in style guide):
	
	  - Data about color values
	  - Typeface sizes/ styles
	  - Logo in color/ black & white
		• Consolidate details from items above.
		
		• Include Cascading Style Sheet to accommodate repeating text elements.
			• Design team

• Collect one current news article.	• Use article from current edition of newspaper.	• Article may need to be shortened to four paragraphs for website.	• Writing team; consult newspaper editors. • Update weekly or bi-weekly depending on timeliness of news.
• Collect photo for current article.	• Get digital photo from newspaper or scan original if necessary.	• Photo needs to be optimized, edited, cropped, and saved as JPEG to fit into article page ($<$ 65K).	• Design team and newspaper staff • Update weekly or bi-weekly depending on timeliness of news.
• Collect two articles for archive section.	• Use articles from previous edition of newspaper.	• Articles need to be shortened to four paragraphs for website. • Two articles (archive 1 and archive 2 pages)	• Writing team; consult newspaper editors. • Update with "current news" articles.
• Collect photos for two archive articles.	• Get digital photo from newspaper or scan original if necessary.	• Photos may need to be sharpened, brightness/contrast adjusted, cropped, and saved as JPEG to fit into archive pages.	• Writing team; consult newspaper photographers. • Update with "current news" photos.
• Write up calendar for school events in current month.	• List of events in current month	• Create an HTML table to display calendar.	• Writing team; consult vice principal for student activities. • Update monthly.

Job	Materials	Details	Assigned to/ Update Schedule
• Write up calendar for athletic events in current month.	• List of events in current month	• Create an HTML table to display calendar.	• Writing team; consult athletic director for student activities. • Update monthly.
• Create alumni list for year 2001.	• Get word-processed list to save time.	• Implement mailto: tags.	• Writing team; consult alumni contact at school. • Compile annually; update biannually.
• Write article about alumni activities.	• Limit to four paragraphs.	• Create HTML page.	• Writing team; consult contact at school. • Update according to alumni meetings.
• Create list of program of studies.	• List of class/course name	• Create HTML page.	• Writing team; consult vice principal for curriculum. • Update each semester.
• Create list of special programs.	• List of class/course names	• Create HTML pages.	• Writing team; consult special programs teacher. • Update each semester.
• Create list of staff sorted by faculty (list of phone, address, e-mail of staff members).	• List of teachers, word-processed or text-only with e-mail links and phone numbers	• Implement mailto: tags.	• Writing team; consult principal. • Compile annually; update as needed.
• Create contact form with text fields, check boxes, and radio buttons (used to contact school staff about grants, documentation requests, and the like).	•	• Include JavaScript script to evaluate form.	• Program team. • Check at least twice a week for messages; respond within 24 hours.

Here's how to make GoLive build the site's flowchart:

1. Double-click the website icon of the completed Washington High School website.

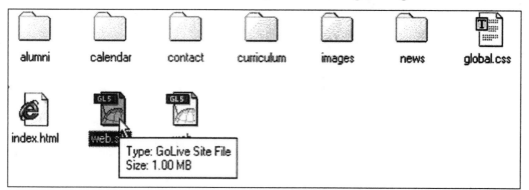

2. After GoLive is launched with the Washington High School website, click the

   Navigation View button 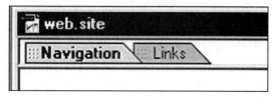.

3. A new window opens with the Navigation tab selected.

4. Click the Maximize button at the top of the window, and scroll through the page to see that the structure of the construction and navigation of the site is pictured as you had planned it.

5. Select the Page Setup window from the File menu and select Portrait. You ensure that this orientation is selected because the flowchart is displayed vertically.

6. Select File, Print to print your flowchart. It might be helpful to print your chart with the branches of your site collapsed, like this.

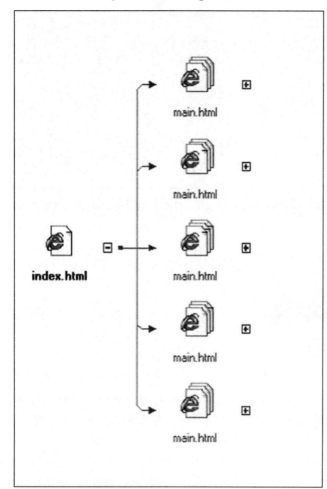

Of course, you can expand all the branches of the site and print its flowchart on two pages, as shown here.

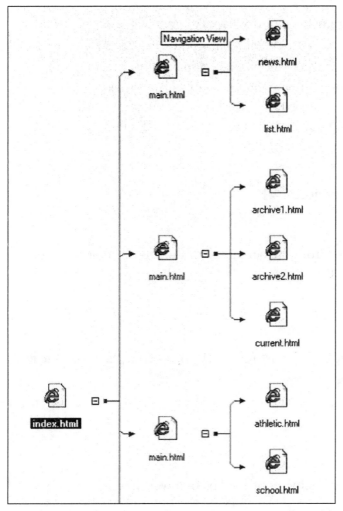

In this lab, you considered your site's features and functions carefully, and now the requirements document and site plan will help guide you and your client, Washington High School, to a useful and functional web presence.

Check Your Understanding

1. What is the correct sequence of the pre-production phase?

   A. Proposal development, brainstorming session, contract negotiation
   B. Brainstorming session, proposal development, contract negotiation
   C. Contract negotiation, proposal development, brainstorming session
   D. Proposal development, contract negotiation, brainstorming session

2. Which of the following should you do when working with clients?

   A. Prepare for meetings.
   B. Listen to the client.
   C. Show enthusiasm for the project.
   D. All of the above.

3. You should let the client know from the beginning of the process that his or her input is essential for the project to succeed.

   A. True
   B. False

4. When creating a website, who is the most important member of the project team?

   A. Project manager
   B. Web designer
   C. Client
   D. No one

5. What is one of the determining factors in the scope of a website?

   A. The designer's newest design tool
   B. Features of the WYSIWYG editor
   C. The length of the domain name
   D. Client's budget constraints

6. Which of the following determines how a user can find and access information?

   A. Requirements document
   B. Task sequencing
   C. Scope definition
   D. Information architecture

7. Media files (for example, GIF, JPEG, SWF) are embedded within HTML pages appearing as graphics, animations, and videos.

   A. True
   B. False

8. What is information architecture?

    A. A content update plan
    B. A database-driven website
    C. Your client's marketing collateral
    D. The organization of content

9. What is a dynamic website?

    A. Database-driven
    B. Full of animations
    C. Updated content
    D. Uses the latest technology

10. Which document would provide an opportunity for you to get your client's signature?

    A. Site flowchart
    B. Information architecture
    C. Requirements document
    D. Cost estimate

11. The web designer assesses the needs of the client during the proposal.

    A. True
    B. False

12. Which phase includes interviewing the client and preparing a proposal?

    A. Pre-production
    B. Production
    C. Post-production
    D. None of the above

13. What is the most viable method of media storage?

    A. CD-ROM
    B. Zip disk
    C. Hard drive
    D. All of the above

14. How your client defines the audience of the website will not have a significant impact on how you design.

    A. True
    B. False

15. What is the scheduling tool that identifies and documents the interactivity dependencies?

    A. Task sequencing
    B. Vision statement
    C. Scope planning
    D. Resource planning

16. You need to determine the time and budget constraints of the client during the pre-production phase.

    A. True
    B. False

17. Which of the following includes a list of what the client needs to provide a web designer and a detailed, revised flowchart?

    A. Site flowchart
    B. Scope definition
    C. Proposal
    D. Requirements document

18. Researching the client's business, explaining the design process, and showing enthusiasm are all examples of which of the following?

    A. Audience definition
    B. Project management
    C. File management
    D. Client management

19. Audio obtained from the client can be converted to formats that you can use for the web using a sound card and an audio-editing program.

    A. True
    B. False

20. Which of the following are types of files that you can edit within Adobe GoLive?

    A. SWF and AVI
    B. SWF and WAV
    C. PSD and LIV
    D. AVI and WAV

Chapter 5
Layout and Design

Introduction

Design is the organization of visual information. Design principles are descriptions of how we can better organize visual information. In this chapter, you look at how web designers use clarity, consistency, contrast, simplicity, structure, and emphasis to make their designs work.

In addition, you see how different web designers present a website to the user for the first time. The first page of a website is either a home page or splash page. A *home page* gives information about the site and navigation buttons or links to each section within the site. Frequently, home pages are used to give the latest news about a company or product. *Splash pages*, on the other hand, are predominantly graphical and animated in nature. Splash pages are common for product websites, often showcasing the product by flashy, colorful, or unusual effects. Users can sometimes skip the animation in a splash page and go to a page that provides navigational links and textual content.

The five labs in this chapter show you how to export images to a web format, create navigation buttons, create rollover navigation buttons, create a project site and page templates, and create a style sheet. You use Adobe GoLive and Photoshop for these labs.

Focus Questions

1. What are the three opportunities that a web designer has to "hook" users when they first enter the website?

   _____

   _____

2. If you want to emphasize a certain element, say the sale price of a product, what are some of the ways that you can draw attention to it?

   _____

   _____

3. How can you make a website have clarity?

   _____

   _____

4. What monitor coordinates are used as the point of origin by Internet Explorer? Netscape Navigator?

   _____

   _____

5. How do a browser's point-of-origin coordinates affect the outcome of your design?

_____

_____

6. What aspects of monitors can make a web page appear differently from user to user?

_____

_____

7. What is the recommended method for adding a background color to your website?

_____

_____

8. Why would you want to choose common fonts for your website?

_____

_____

9. How are frames used?

_____

_____

10. What is usually placed in a static frame?

_____

_____

Discovery Exercises

Splash Pages

Go to www.turbonium.com to see a splash page.

Can you skip the splash page? _____

What do you like about this splash page? _____

Does this splash page add to the website? _____

What could be improved? _____

Now find other splash pages on the web.

First Splash Page

Can you skip the splash page? _____

What do you like about this splash page?_____

Does this splash page add to the website? _____

What could be improved? _____

Second Splash Page

Can you skip the splash page? _____

What do you like about this splash page?_____

Does this splash page add to the website? _____

What could be improved? _____

Design Principles

Go to three sites that advertise similar product like www.coca-cola.com, www.drpepper.com, and www.7up.com. For each of these sites, evaluate how the web designers handled each design principle and whether it is successful.

First Site

URL: _____

Clarity: _____

Consistency and Unity: _____

Contrast: _____

Simplicity: _____

Structure: _____

Emphasis: _____

Overall analysis of site: _____

What can be improved? _____

Second Site

URL: _____

Clarity: _____

Consistency and Unity: _____

Contrast: _____

Simplicity: _____

Structure: _____

Emphasis: _____

Overall analysis of site: _____

What can be improved? _____

Third Site

URL: _____

Clarity: _____

Consistency and Unity: _____

Contrast: _____

Simplicity: _____

Structure: _____

Emphasi: _____

Overall analysis of site: _____

What can be improved? _____

Emphasis

One way to make something stand out is to restrict your color palette to just a few colors. Then when you want something to stand out, use a contrasting color. Similarly, you can use a different font, size, weight, or other stylistic change. Go to www.mtv.com. How does the web designer use emphasis?

_____

_____

_____

How could the web designer improve emphasis on the website?

_____

_____

_____

_____

Consistency

Check out three of your favorite sites. Do they use elements like color, placement of hyperlinks, placement of home page icon, consistently?

First Site

URL: _____

Are the navigation buttons in the same place on every page? _____

Are the navigation buttons and headers consistently named? _____

If color is used to indicate sections, is it used consistently? _____

Is the logo used as a link to the home page? _____

What needs to be changed so that the site has consistency? _____

_____

Second Site

URL: _____

Are the navigation buttons in the same place on every page? _____

Are the navigation buttons and headers consistently named? _____

If color is used to indicate sections, is it used consistently? _____

Is the logo used as a link to the home page? _____

What needs to be changed so that the site has consistency? _____

_____

Third Site

URL: _____

Are the navigation buttons in the same place on every page? _____

Are the navigation buttons and headers consistently named? _____

If color is used to indicate sections, is it used consistently? _____

Is the logo used as a link to the home page? _____

What needs to be changed so that the site has consistency? _____

_____

Lab 5.1: Exporting to Web Format (Photoshop)

In this lab, you create a web-ready image file for your web page header. This is based on the header.psd that you created in the previous labs.

1. Start Photoshop and open the header.psd from the Course Project folder. If you skipped previous labs, you can find a pre-made header in 4/Start/layout/header.psd on the accompanying CD-ROM.

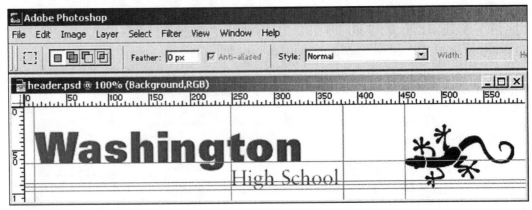

2. Check the image size (image dimensions) to make sure the file is the appropriate size. Do this by choosing the Image, Image Size menu item.

3.　In the Image Size window that appears, you can check the image size and, if necessary, change it. In this case, the size is 600 x 110 pixels.

```
Image Size                                    [x]

  ┌ Pixel Dimensions: 194K ──────────┐    ┌──────┐
  │                                  │    │  OK  │
  │   Width:  [600]   [pixels    ▼]┐ │    └──────┘
  │                               ]⊗│    ┌──────┐
  │   Height: [110]   [pixels    ▼]┘ │    │Cancel│
  │                                  │    └──────┘
  └──────────────────────────────────┘    ┌──────┐
  ┌ Document Size: ──────────────────┐     │ Auto.│
  │                                  │     └──────┘
  │   Width:  [8.333]   [inches   ▼]┐ │
  │                                ]⊗│
  │   Height: [1.528]   [inches   ▼]┘ │
  │                                  │
  │  Resolution: [72]   [pixels/inch ▼]│
  └──────────────────────────────────┘
     ☑ Constrain Proportions
     ☑ Resample Image: [Bicubic        ▼]
```

4.　Click OK to exit out of this window.

5.　Take note of the physical file size of your image file. There are two methods:

- The first method is to click the triangle at the bottom-left border of the Photoshop window. Make sure that Document Sizes is the current view option. The number on the left represents the printing size of header.psd (with all layers flattened). The number on the right indicates the file size, including all layers.

- The second method uses your File Explorer. If you right-click the File icon and select Properties (a), you will be shown the Properties window (b) that tells you about the physical file size.

Using either method, you can see that the header.psd has a size of 107 KB.

a)

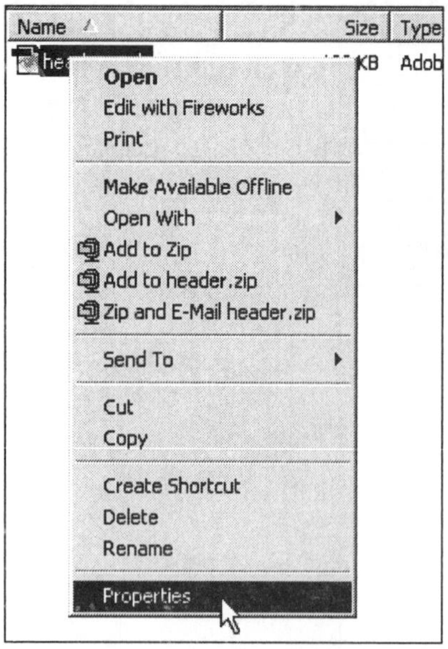

b)

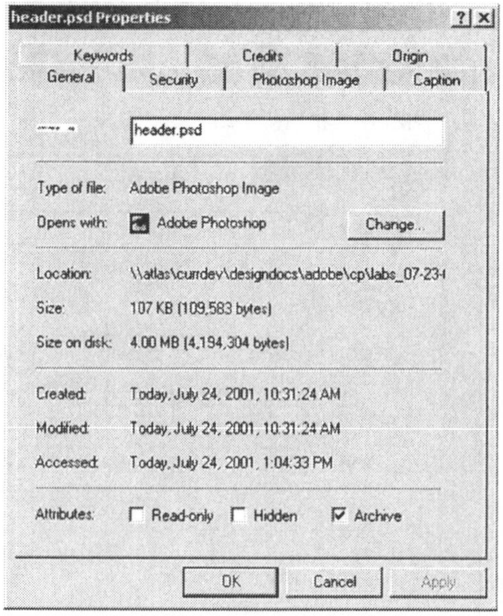

6. Because .psd is not a format allowed on a web page, you need to export the header.psd to a web format, such as GIF or JPEG. Because the header consists of simple colored objects with no gradients or photo-realistic imagery, the best format to use is GIF.

7. Photoshop offers a Save for Web option that can be found under the menu item File. Select File, Save for Web from the menu bar.

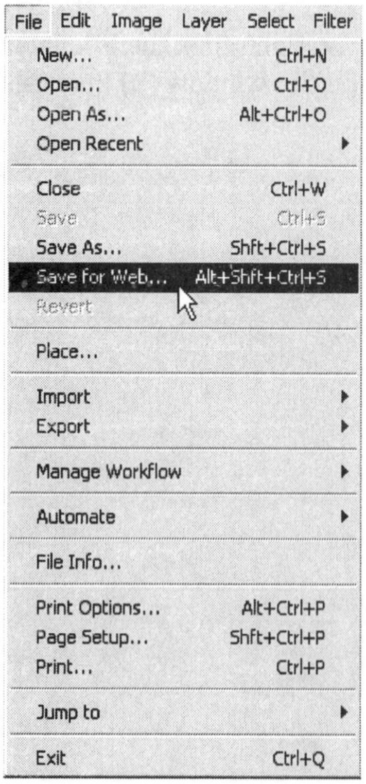

8. A new window appears and shows the Save for Web options. You will find the file size information in the lower-left corner of each version of the image. The Original tab shows the original .psd file, its file size, and color palette without any optimization changes.

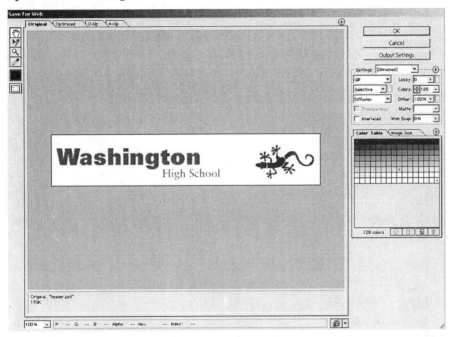

9. The last tab is titled 4-Up. By clicking this tab, you see a screen with four images: the original and three versions of optimized GIFs. If you need to change the image format to GIF, it can be selected in the drop-down menu to the right of the Preview window. The difference between these GIF versions is the numbers of colors in their color palettes, as you can see from the text at the lower right of the image samples:

- Original, header.psd, 193 K

- GIF, 8.466 K, 4 sec @ 28.8 Kbps, 100% dither, Selective palette, 128 colors

- GIF, 7.772 K, 4 sec @ 28.8 Kbps, 100% dither, Selective palette, 64 colors

- GIF, 8.466 K, 4 sec @ 28.8 Kbps, 0% dither, Selective palette, 128 colors

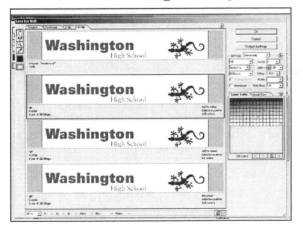

Note: The options shown in your Preview window might differ; they can be changed in the Settings options next to the Preview window.

10. You can now examine the options closely by zooming in on them to determine which option will offer the best quality and the highest reduction in file size. Photoshop also preselects an option for you, which is the one with the black border around it. In this case, the second option offers better quality with only a slight larger file size. The difference between this choice and Photoshop's is only 0.7 KB. Because this is such a small difference in file size, we'll go with the higher-quality choice (choice #2).

11. To export this choice, make sure that the second sample is selected by clicking it and then clicking OK to export the file.

12. Save the file as header.gif in the Course Project folder.

13. Also create a folder called web on your hard drive; this is where you will actually set up your website structure. Within the web folder, you will create a folder called images, within which you will create a subfolder called header. In this header folder, you will copy and paste your header.gif file.

Lab 5.2: Creating Navigation Buttons (Photoshop)

In this lab, you learn to use Adobe Photoshop to create the navigation buttons for your web page. Because these buttons will have a rollover effect, in reality, you will be creating three versions of the same button. In later labs, you will create the other necessary buttons and learn how to combine these buttons to create a mouseover effect for your web page.

1. Open Photoshop. Choose File, New from the upper taskbar. When the New dialog box opens, name the new file buttons, and enter the dimensions width 121, height 25 pixels, and resolution 72 pixels/inch.

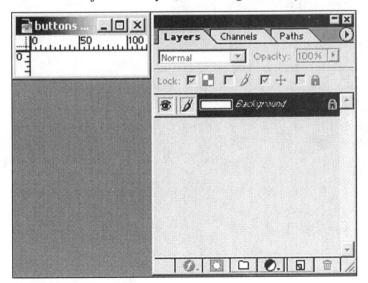

2. This file has just one layer, the background layer, which is white.

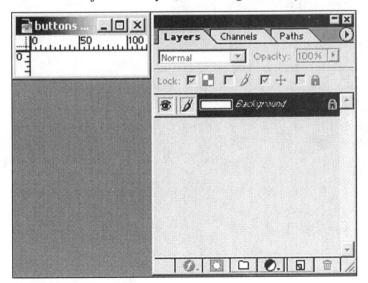

3. In the toolbox , click the Foreground Color area to choose a color.

4. Set the color to RGB: 102, 153, 204 (note that this is a web-safe color).

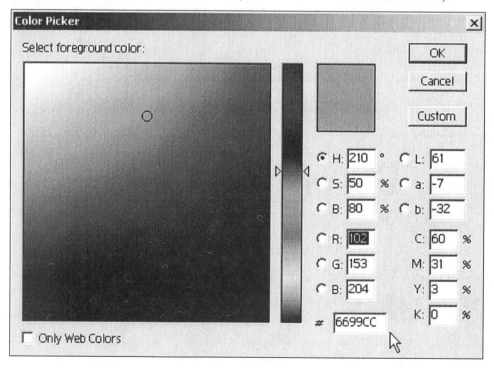

5. To fill the background layer with the selected foreground color, go to the menu item Edit, Fill and, in the Fill Option window, choose from the drop-down button Foreground Color and click OK.

6. The fill background is now light blue.

7. Now you need to set the foreground color to white (RGB: 255,255,255).

8. Select the Type tool from the toolbox. Place the cursor in the button area, and type "NEWS" (note the capitalization). The font specifications to use for the button captions are the following:

Univers, 67 Condensed Bold, 16 pt, Crisp, Centered

Note: If these font options are not available to you, choose another sans serif font.

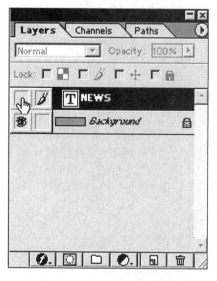

9. To adjust the tracking space, go to the Window, Show Character menu item. In the Character palette, adjust the tracking to –50. Click the checkmark in the tool options bar to commit the changes.

10. Save your file as buttons.psd in the Course Project folder.

11. Hide your News Type Layer by clicking the eye in your Layers palette.

12. Select the Type tool from the Tools Palette, place it in the button area, and type CALENDAR.

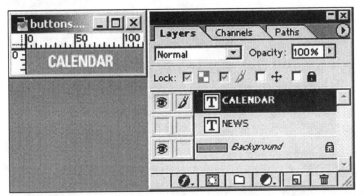

13. Repeat Steps 11 and 12 to create type layers for the words CURRICULUM, ALUMNI, and CONTACT.

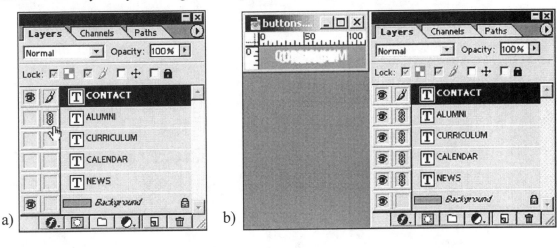

14. Unhide all type layers. Make sure that the Contact layer is the current selection. Link all the other layers by clicking in the square on the right, as shown in a) and b).

15. Align all type layers at the bottom ▣, and center them horizontally ▣ by selecting the Move tool and then using the Align Option buttons that appears in the tool option bar (beneath the menu bar at the top of the Program window).

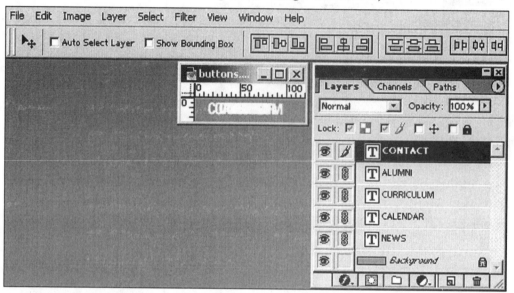

16. Now hide all type layers except for the longest (CURRICULUM).

17. Open the Info palette by selecting the menu item Window, Show Info.

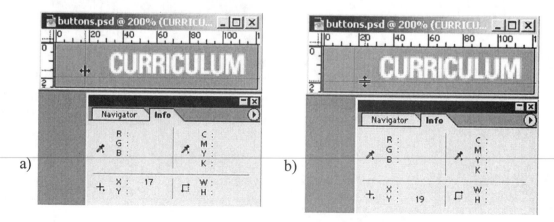

The Info palette shows, for example, the coordinates of the mouse over the image surface.

18. If you need to display the rulers, select View, Show Rulers from the menu bar. Next, create a vertical guide at 17 pixels (X coordinate—watch the lower-right quarter of the Info tab) and a horizontal guide at 19 pixels (Y coordinate). You might need to zoom in to better view the selection. The following figures show the resulting a) vertical guide and b) horizontal guide.

19. Check to see that the View, Snap to Guides is turned on. Click the Curriculum layer in the Layers palette to select it. Then select the Move tool and drag the Curriculum layer (and all layers linked to it) so that the left and bottom border align with the guides and snap to them.

20. Save your file.

   With this, you have centered all your type layers consistently in the center of the button area.

21. Now it's time to create the border of the buttons. To do this, create a new layer by clicking the palette option menu (black arrow in the top-left corner of the Layers palette) and selecting the New Layer option.

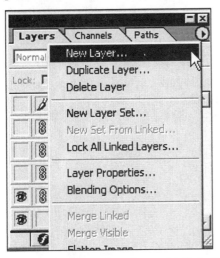

   Name the layer border and click OK.

22. Change the foreground color to RGB: 204,204,204.

Color Picker

Select foreground color:

[ ] OK
[ ] Cancel
[ ] Custom

- H: 0 °
- S: 0 %
- B: 80 %
- R: 204
- G: 204
- B: 204
- # CCCCCC

- L: 82
- a: 0
- b: 0
- C: 19 %
- M: 15 %
- Y: 15 %
- K: 0 %

[ ] Only Web Colors

23. Select the Pencil tool from your toolbox. (The pencil can be hidden under the paintbrush tool. If so, hold the left mouse button on the paintbrush tool and click the pencil tool.) Change the brush width to 1 in the tool options bar.

File   Edit   Image   Layer   Select   Filter   View   Window   Help

Brush: 1   Mode: Normal   Opacity: 100%   ☐ Auto Erase

24. Place the pencil in the bottom-left corner of your button area and hold down the Shift key. Now drag the mouse right until you reach the right border of the button area. Holding down the Shift key enables you to draw straight horizontal or vertical lines (you might want to zoom in to make this easier).

25. Draw a vertical border line from the bottom-right corner to the top-right corner while holding down the Shift key.

26. Save your file.

27. Now hide all type layers but the Contact layer.

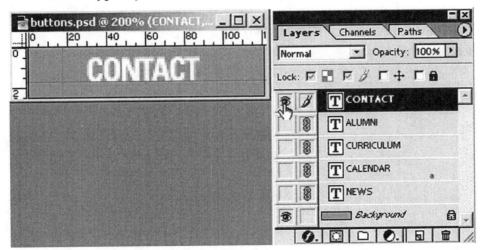

28. To create the contact navigation button, go to the File, Save for Web menu item.

File Edit Image Layer Select Filter

New...	Ctrl+N
Open...	Ctrl+O
Open As...	Alt+Ctrl+O
Open Recent	▶
Close	Ctrl+W
Save	Ctrl+S
Save As...	Shft+Ctrl+S
Save for Web...	Alt+Shft+Ctrl+S
Revert	
Place...	
Import	▶
Export	▶
Manage Workflow	▶
Automate	▶
File Info...	
Print Options...	Alt+Ctrl+P
Page Setup...	Shft+Ctrl+P
Print...	Ctrl+P
Jump to	▶
Exit	Ctrl+Q

29. Ensure that the Contact layer at the top of the layer stack is unhidden. In the Save for Web window, you will again see the 4-Up image samples. Because this is a small image with only a few colors, there is basically just one choice of color palette to create an optimized image; that is why you will see the same option three times: GIF, 518 bytes, 1 sec @ 28.8 Kbps, 100% dither, Selective palette, 17 colors.

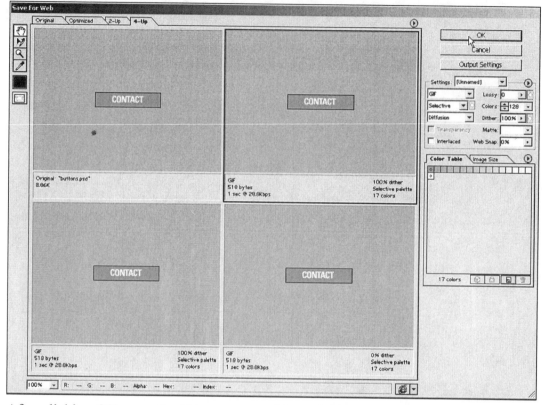

30. After clicking OK, save the file as contact.gif in a folder called navigation, which is within your images folder. You need to create the folder called navigation within your images folder.

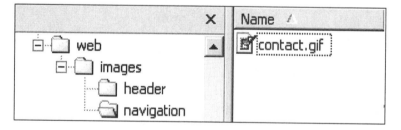

31. Hide the Contact layer and show the Alumni layer.

32. Go to File, Save for Web and save the file as alumni.gif in the navigation folder.

33. Repeat Step 26 for the Curriculum layer (create curriculum.gif), the Calendar layer (create calendar.gif), and the News layer (create news.gif). After you finish, the file structure for your web folder looks like this.

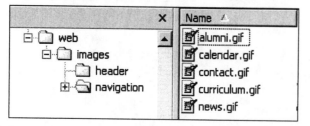

34. Save your buttons.psd file to your Course Project folder for future reference.

Lab 5.3: Creating Rollover Navigation Buttons (Photoshop)

In this lab, you learn to use Adobe Photoshop to create the rollover buttons for the navigation of your web page.

1. Open Photoshop and open the file called buttons.psd from your Course Project folder.

2. Save this file as buttonsov.psd in your Course Project folder.

3. In the Layers palette, select New Layer from the Palette option menu and name it Contact BG. Click OK.

4. Drag this layer so it is below the Contact Type layer.

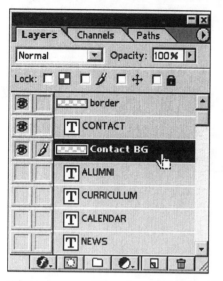

5. Change your fill color to RGB: 102,102,0, and activate the Contact BG layer. Select the layer by choosing Select, All or by holding the option key and clicking on the Contact BG layer. Use the Paintbucket tool (located under the Gradient tool) to fill the Contact BG layer with the new foreground color. Ensure that the eye icon is chosen for the border and the Contact layers.

6. Your result looks like this.

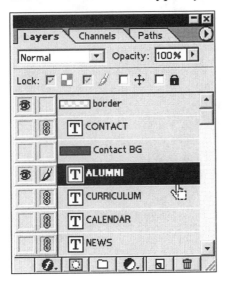

7. Save your file.

8. Select the Alumni Type layer by clicking it. Hide the Contact Type and BG layers, and show the Alumni Type layer.

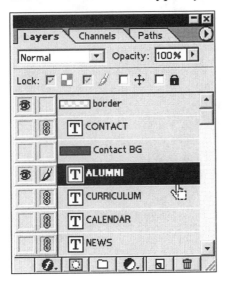

9. Now create a new layer, name it Alumni BG, and drag it below the Alumni Type layer.

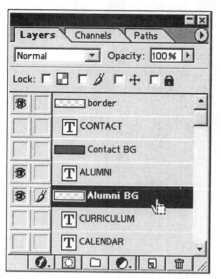

10. Select the entire area of the layer (Select, All or Option-click the layer). Change your foreground color to RGB: 0,102,102 and use the Paintbucket tool to fill the Alumni BG layer with this color.

11. Repeat Steps 7 through 10 for the Curriculum, Calendar, and News layers, using these RGB values:

   • Curriculum RGB: 153,0,102

   • Calendar RGB: 204,51,0

   • News RGB: 255,102,0

12. Save your file.

13. Your result looks like this.

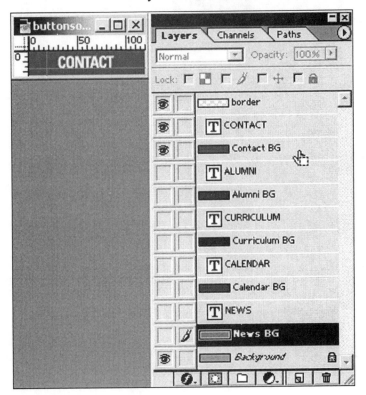

14. Now you can export the button images for the rollover states. Start by hiding the News Type and BG layers, and showing the Contact Type and BG layers. Also, make sure that the Border layer is not hidden.

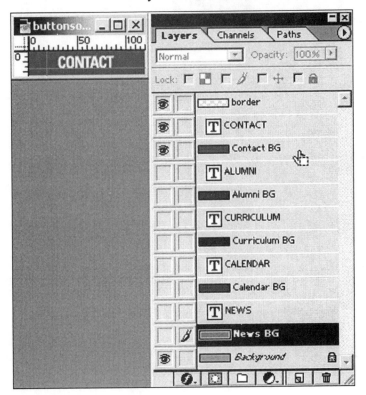

15. Save this image for the web (File, Save for Web) under the name contactov.gif in your web folder. (The path is web/images/navigation/contactov.gif.)

16. Hide the two Contact layers, and unhide the Alumni layers.

17. You can now save this image for the web (File, Save for Web) under web/images/navigation/alumniov.gif.

18. Repeat Steps 16 and 17 to create the files curriculumov.gif, calendarov.gif, and newsov.gif. Your web/images/navigation folder should look like this afterwards.

19. Save your file as buttonsov.psd.

20. Save the same file (File, Save As) under the name buttonsdn.psd in your layout folder.

21. In the Layers window of buttonsdn.psd, select the News Type layer by clicking it.

22. Select the Move tool from the toolbox.

23. This action activates all linked layers–the chain icons show up. By using the arrow keys, move the type layers two pixels down (tap the down-arrow key twice) and two pixels to the right (tap the right-arrow key twice).

Before:

After:

24. Save your file.

25. With the border, NEWS type, and News BG unhidden, save the image for the web under the name in the navigation folder. Call it newsdn.gif.

26. Hide the two News layers and unhide the two Contact layers. Then save the image for the web in the navigation folder, and name it contactdn.gif.

27. Repeat the steps for the rest of the layers to create the files alumnidn.gif, curriculumdn.gif, and calendardn.gif.

28. Save buttonsdn.psd.

You have successfully created a normal, an over, and a down button for all five rollover navigation buttons.

Lab 5.4: Creating a Project Site and Page Templates (GoLive)

In this lab, you learn to create a project site using GoLive. You also learn how to set up your project site using the page template that you constructed in the earlier lab. Furthermore, you set up more sophisticated page templates for your home, main section, and subsection pages.

Remember: A website is an evolving entity unto itself. It keeps changing as information, graphics, animations, and other elements are added.

1. If you are using a PC, copy and paste your existing page template that you created in Lab 1 into the web folder and rename it index.html. After you are finished, close the folder. On the Mac, press the Option key, select the file, and drag-and-drop the file into the appropriate folder.

2. Open Adobe GoLive.

3. When GoLive opens, it automatically gives you a new page. Close this page.

4. Go to your upper taskbar, and choose File, New Site, Import from Folder.

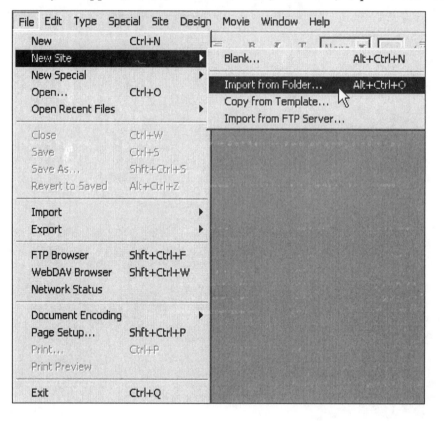

5. After the Import New Project dialog box appears, browse to your index.html file.

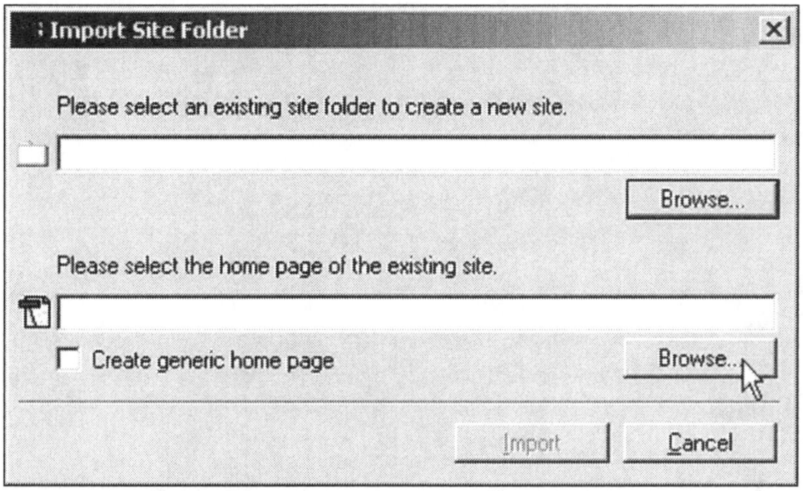

6. The lower text field box prompts you to select a home page for the existing site. Browse to your web folder and choose index.html. When working on a Mac, the icon for the index.html file is a GoLive icon as opposed to the Internet Explorer icon seen by PC users (and shown in the following figure). Click Open.

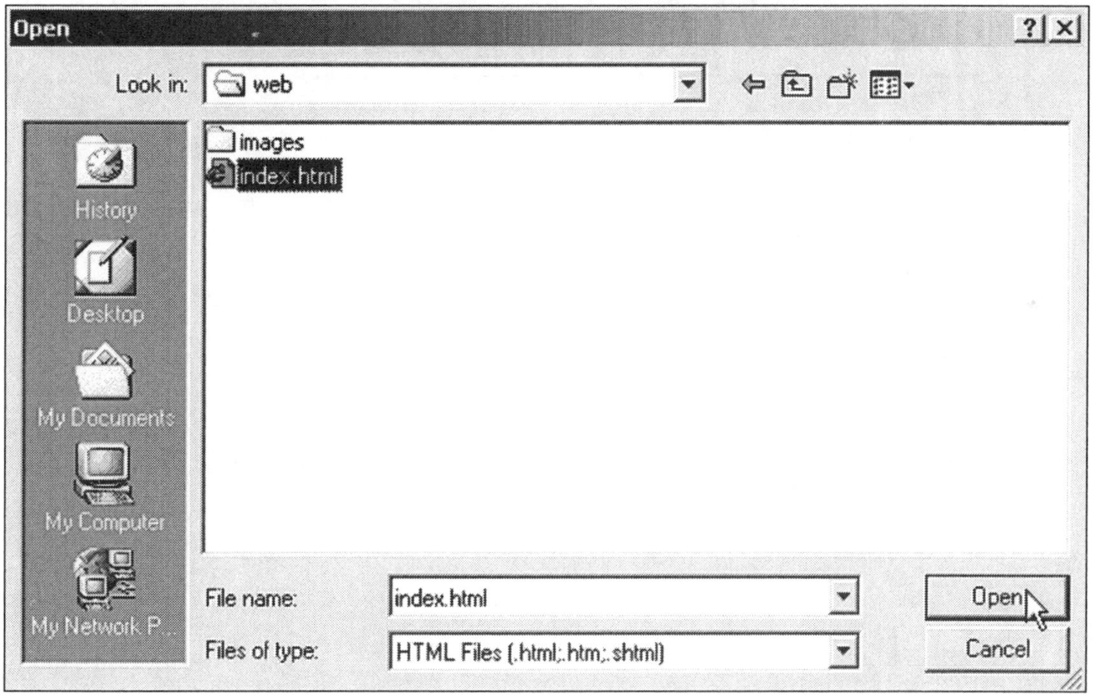

7. Click Import.

8. GoLive now asks you to choose a folder and a filename for the GoLive site document to store the site data. Choose the web folder so your website will be stored in this folder.

9. Click Save.

10. GoLive creates a new project site and imports any folders that were nested in the web folder. For example, this project consists of three items: the images folder (that contains your navigation folder with all the rollover images and the header image), the index.html page, and the web.site GoLive project file. Mac users will only see two files, the images folder and the index.html file, both with GoLive icons.

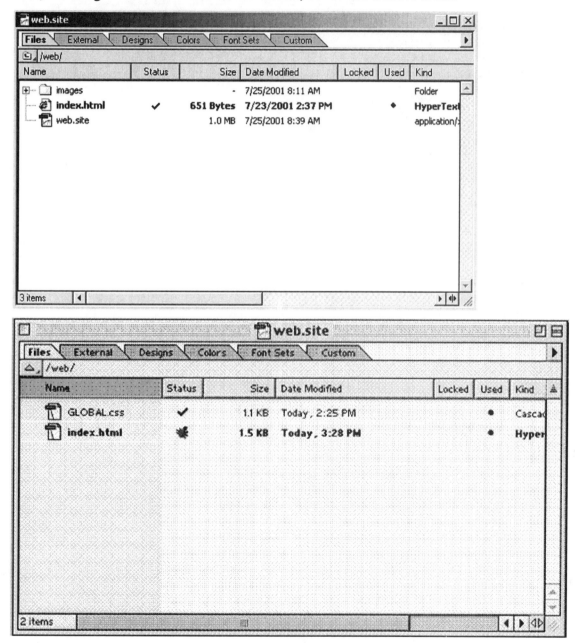

11. Open the index.html page by double-clicking the File icon.

12. This basic page template will now be modified to accommodate all necessary cells for the site's pages. Start by placing your cursor in the cell that says Content. Delete this word and create another nested table (as shown in Figure b) in the content cell by dragging over the Table icon ▯ from the Objects window (as shown in Figure a).

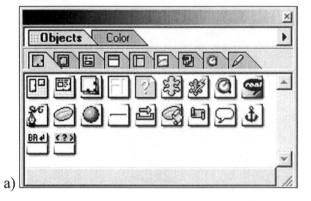

a)

b)

13. You need to adjust the default settings for the new table. For this, you must use the
Inspector window that shows the table properties whenever the table is active
(it has been selected). Modify the Inspector's Table tab to show the following
specifications.

14. In the new nested table, select the left-top table cell by clicking its lower border; it turns light gray, and appears a bit raised to indicate that it's active.

15. At the same time, the display of the Inspector window brings the Cell tab to the front, showing the properties of the selected cell. Change the properties to show the following specifications.

16. Your table should look like this now.

17. Click in the cell and enter the word Icon in the edited table cell for better recognition.

Header						
Navigation						
Subheader						
Icon						
Footer						

18. Now select the bottom right cell of the nested table by clicking one of its borders (or you can right-click in the cell and choose Select Cell from the pop-up menu).

Header						
Navigation						
Subheader						
Icon						
Footer						

19. Be careful to select the correct cell. Your Inspector window should show this Cell tab now.

Inspector	View Controller

| Table | Row | Cell |

Vertical Alignment   Default

Horizontal Alignment   Default

Row Span   1   □ Color

Column Span   1

Width   Auto

Height   Auto

□ Header Style   □ No Text Wrap

□ BgImage

Add Row/Column

Delete Row/Column

Table

20. Change the Vertical Alignment of this cell to Top.

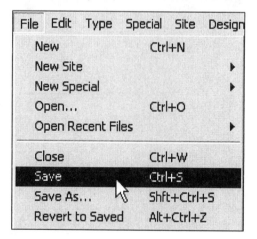

21. After that, click in the cell and add the words Page Content to this cell for future reference.

22. Choose File, Save from the menu bar to save the index.html file.

23. Close the index.html window, and save the changes to the index.html file.

24. In the website window, create a new folder by right-clicking (PC) or control-clicking (Mac) in the white space and choosing the New Folder option from the menu.

25. Name this folder news. Create four other folders called calendar, curriculum, alumni, and contact. The result should look like this.

26. In the same window, right-click (PC) or control-click (Mac) on the index.html file and choose Duplicate from the context menu. Rename the new file to indes1.html.

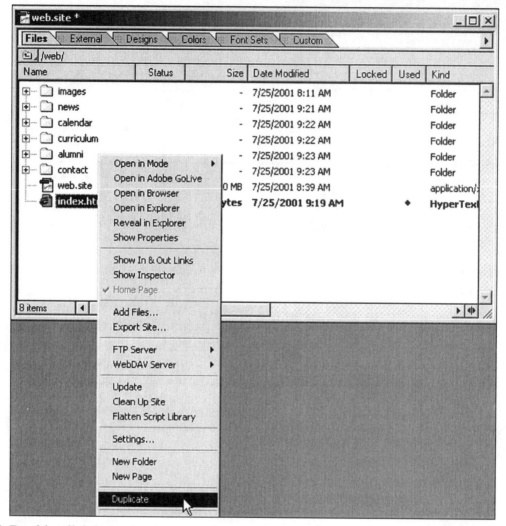

27. Double-click index.html to open it.

28. Select the Icon Cell of the nested table and then select the Table tab in the Inspector window.

29. Now modify the cell layout of the nested table by changing the specifications under the Table tab to Rows 4 and Columns 4. The result looks like this.

30. In the nested table, activate the second cell from the left in the first row by clicking its border (*Note*: It might be helpful to hold the Shift key down and click the bottom border of the cell you're activating).

Header
Navigation
Subheader
Icon
Page Content
Footer

31. In the Inspector window, Cell tab, change the Column Span to 3 with this result.

Header
Navigation
Subheader
Icon
Page Content
Footer

32. Apply the same column span to the cell directly beneath it.

Header
Navigation
Subheader
Icon
Page Content
Footer

33. In the nested table, select the third cell from the left in the third row and apply a row span of 2.

34. Apply the same row span to the fourth cell in this row.

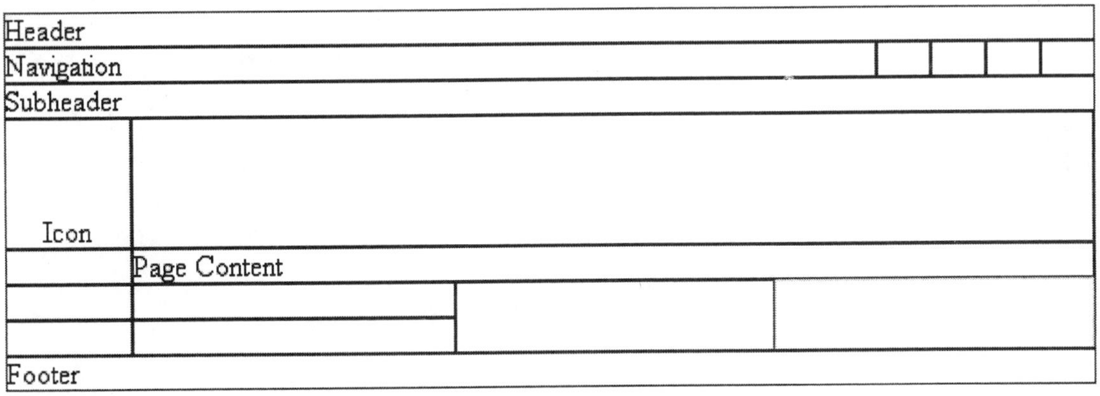

35. Save your file.

36. To make adding content easier in a later lab, insert the cell captions as shown here.

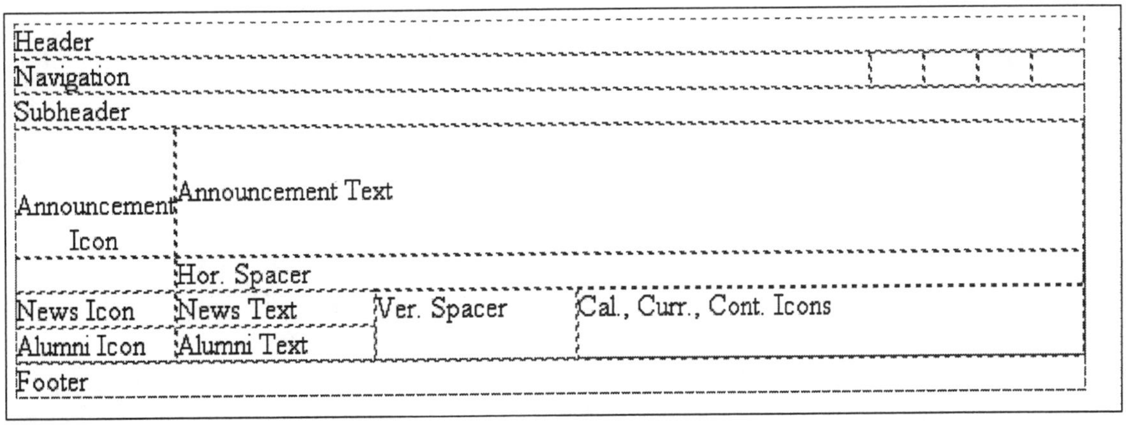

37. After you're done, change the cell properties of the News Icon Cell to Vertical Alignment: Top and Horizontal Alignment: Center.

38. Apply the same to the Alumni Icon Cell.

Header						
Navigation						
Subheader						
Announcement Icon	Announcement Text					
	Hor. Spacer					
News Icon	News Text	Ver. Spacer	Cal., Curr., Cont. Icons			
Alumni Icon	Alumni Text					
Footer						

39. You have now completed the home page template. Close this window and save the file.

40. Save the complete project by clicking File, Save.

Lab 5.5: Creating a Style Sheet (GoLive)

To create a style sheet, you must first define it as an internal or external style sheet; that is, either in the head section of a web page or as a separate file. In this lab, you define an external style sheet that controls all style and formatting for all web pages within your site.

After you define the style sheet, you need to create styles and define properties for the styles. Then you reference it from your page. Finally, you apply the styles to your page elements.

1. Start Adobe GoLive and open your website by selecting File, Open and choosing the web.site file.

2. In the menu bar, choose File, New Special, Style Sheet Document.

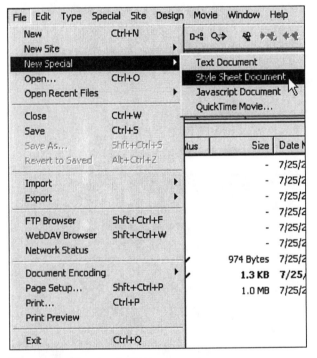

3. The style sheet window appears.

4. Save the style sheet (File, Save As) as global.css in the web root directory. (Mac users will see the web.site and index.html files in addition to those shown here.)

5. Assign all text styles. With the right mouse button (PC) or the control button pressed (Mac), click the gray space within global.css. In the context menu that appears, choose Add Element Selector.

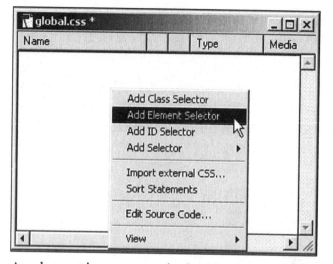

6. An element icon appears in the global.css window. Click the Font tab and the Inspector window will show the element properties that are not yet set.

![Screenshot of global.css window with element selector and Inspector showing Font properties](global.css window with "element" listed. Inspector panel shows Color, Size, Line Height fields, Style: Unchanged, Weight: Unchanged, Decoration options: None, Underline, Strike, Overline, Blink. Font Family box and New button. CSS Selector label.)

7. To enter the name of the element, click the Basic tab 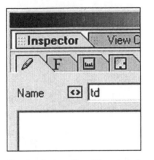 and enter td.

8. Switch to the Font tab.

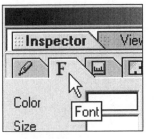

9. Assign Black as the font color by clicking the black arrow next to the Color Field.

144

10. For the font size, click the black arrow next to Size, select Point as the unit, and enter 10 pt.

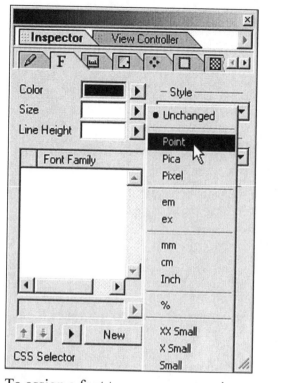

11. To assign a font type, you must assign a common font family by clicking on the black arrow at the bottom of the Inspector Window and selecting Arial, Helvetica, Geneva, Swiss …, as shown here.

12. With that, you have successfully assigned the first style. Save your file.

13. For the second style, you will add a style class that is applied to the td tag. To do this, right-click the style sheet (PC) or click on the style sheet with the control button pressed (Mac) and select Add Class Selector.

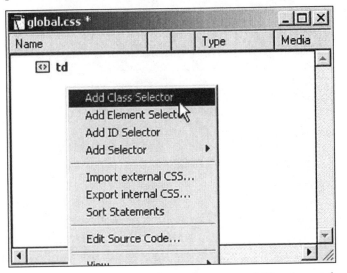

14. In the Basic Tab, enter the style name td.Header and press Enter.

15. In the Font tab, enter the font color White, the font size 16 pt, the font family Arial, Helvetica, Geneva,…," and assign the font weight Bold by using the pull-down button on the right. (Note that Mac users will see a "+" next to Arial, Helvetica, and Geneva in the Font Family menu.)

16. The next style is also a td class and called td.WelcomeHeader. Create the new class selector element like you did before. Click the Font tab and assign a font color by clicking the color square. This opens the Color window.

17. Make sure that the RGB tab is selected .

18. Enter the RGB value 153,204,204; this is a web-safe color represented by 99CCCC in hexadecimal. To apply that color to your new class, activate the class by clicking it in the global.css window and then dragging over the color from the Color window to the Inspector window's Font tab. Drop it into the Color Field.

19. Now apply the following specifications to your class: Size: 16 pt, Font-Family: Arial, Helvetica, Geneva…, Weight: Bold. Your result should look like this figure.

20. Now create the last td class style called td.HomeTable and assign the following specifications: Color: Black, Size: 8 pt, Font Family: Arial, Helvetica,....

21. Save your file.

22. Assign all header formats. To do that, create a new element called h2 and assign theses specifications to it: Font Family: Arial, Helvetica, Geneva..., Color: Gray, Size: 12 pt, Weight: Bold.

23. The next header element to create is called h3 and has the following specifications: Font Family: Arial, Helvetica, ..., Color: Gray, Size: 10 pt, Weight: Bold.

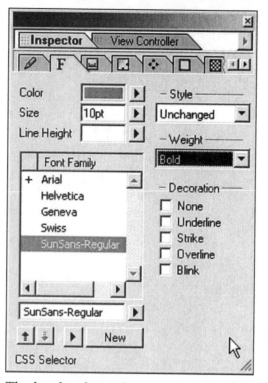

24. The last header style to create is an element called h4 with these specifications. Assign a Font Family: Arial, Helvetica,... Color: Gray, Size: 10 pt, Style: Italic.

25. Save your file.

26. Now assign the hyperlink styles. Start with adding a predefined selector by right-clicking global.css (PC) or control-clicking global.css (Mac), and choosing Add Selector and a:link.

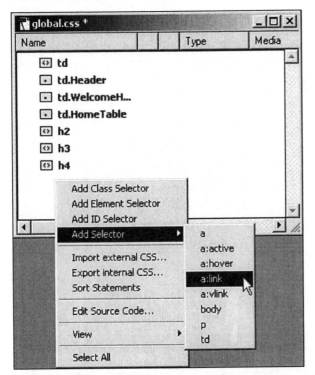

27. In the Inspector window, click the Basic tab, add a comma and a space after "a:link", and add "a:visited, a:active" to the name.

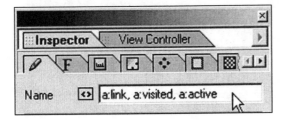

28. Under the Font tab, assign the color Gray to this style.

29. Now add another predefined selector called "a:hover" and assign the font Color RGB value: 192,192,192.

30. You need to create a Class Selector called "a.h1:link, a.h1:visited, a.h1:active." Assign the font Color White to it, as shown in the following figure.

31. Finally, create the last element, a Class Selector, called "a.h1:hover" and assign the Color RGB value: 192,192,192 to it.

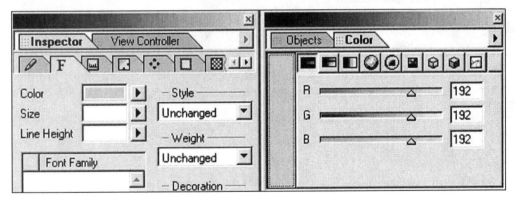

32. You can add the last two styles manually by right-clicking (PC) or control-clicking (Mac) global.css and choosing Edit Source Code.

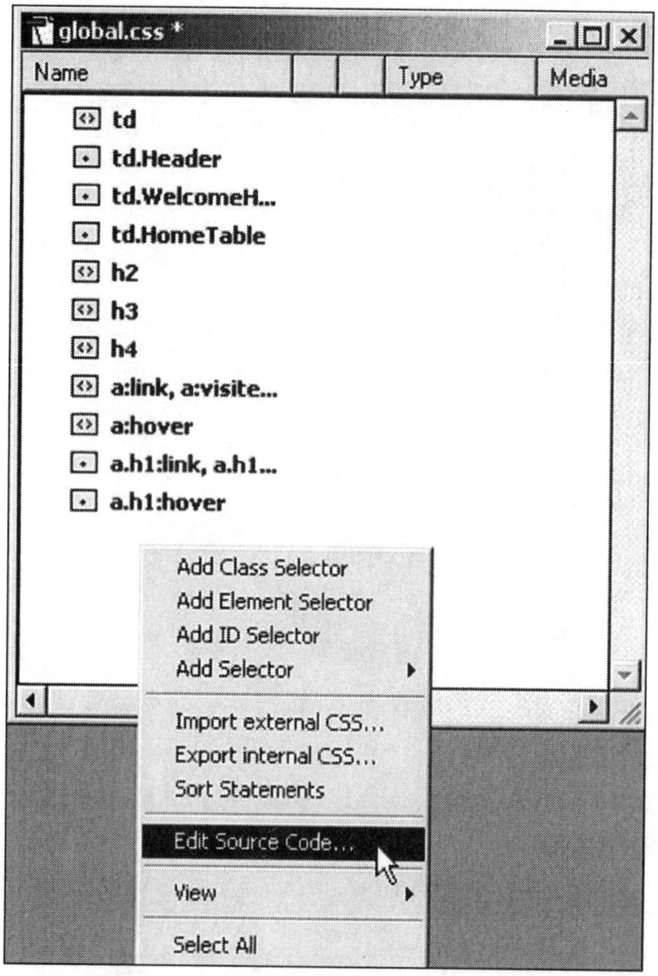

33. In the Editor Tool window (PC) or CSS Source Code window (Mac), scroll to the bottom and add this style code, as shown in the following figure:

```
ul { list-style:disc; }
body { background-color: #ffffff }
```

```
: Tool                                                          [X]

td { color: black; font-size: 10pt; font-family: Arial, Helvetica, Geneva, Swiss, SunSans-F
td.Header { color: white; font-weight: bold; font-size: 16pt; font-family: Arial, Helvetica, G
td.WelcomeHeader { color: #9cc; font-weight: bold; font-size: 16pt; font-family: Arial, Hel
td.HomeTable { color: black; font-size: 8pt; font-family: Arial, Helvetica, Geneva, Swiss, :
h2 { color: gray; font-weight: bold; font-size: 12pt; font-family: Arial, Helvetica, Geneva, S
h3 { color: gray; font-weight: bold; font-size: 10pt; font-family: Arial, Helvetica, Geneva, S
h4 { color: gray; font-style: italic; font-size: 10pt; font-family: Arial, Helvetica, Geneva, Sv
a:link, a:visited, a:active { color: gray }
a:hover { color: #c0c0c0 }
a.h1:link, a.h1:visited, a.h1:active { color: white }
a.h1:hover { color: #c0c0c0 }
ul { list-style:disc; }
body { background-color: #ffffff }

                                              [  OK  ]    [ Cancel ]
```

34. Click OK to commit these edits.

35. Your global.css should now look like this.

```
global.css *                          [_][口][X]
Name                    |    | Type    | Media

    <> td
    [·] td.Header
    [·] td.WelcomeH...
    [·] td.HomeTable
    <> h2
    <> h3
    <> h4
    <> a:link, a:visite...
    <> a:hover
    [·] a.h1:link, a.h1...
    [·] a.h1:hover
    <> ul
    <> body
```

You have now successfully set up an external style sheet that will be used by all the pages in your website.

36. Save your global.css file and close it.

37. You now need to link the external style sheet to your two page templates. To do this, double-click on index.html to open it. Then, in the index.html window, click the CSS Interface button 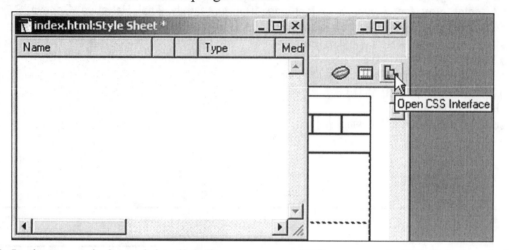 in the top-right corner.

38. In the new window, right-click the gray space (PC) or control-click (Mac) and choose Add Link to External CSS.

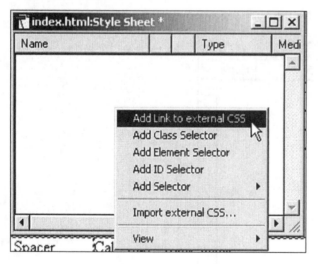

39. After this, an empty reference icon appears in the window. Right-click (PC) or control-click (Mac) on this icon, and choose CSS File, Browse Link, as shown in the following figure.

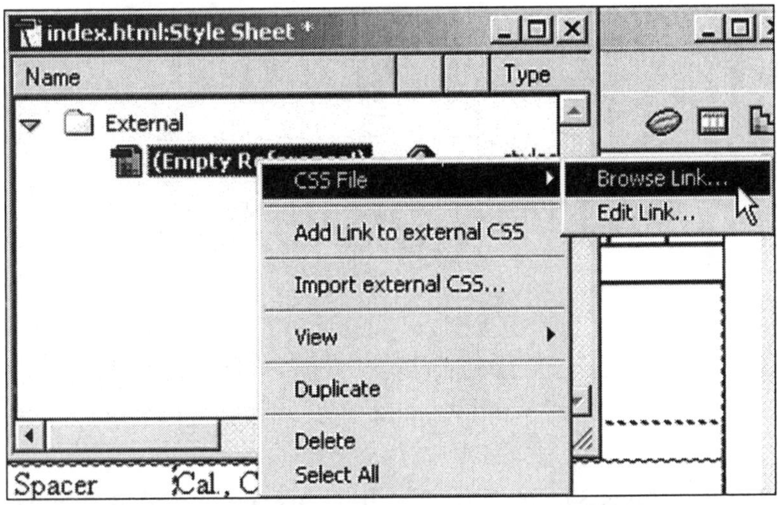

40. Browse to the root directory of your web folder and select global.css. Click Open.

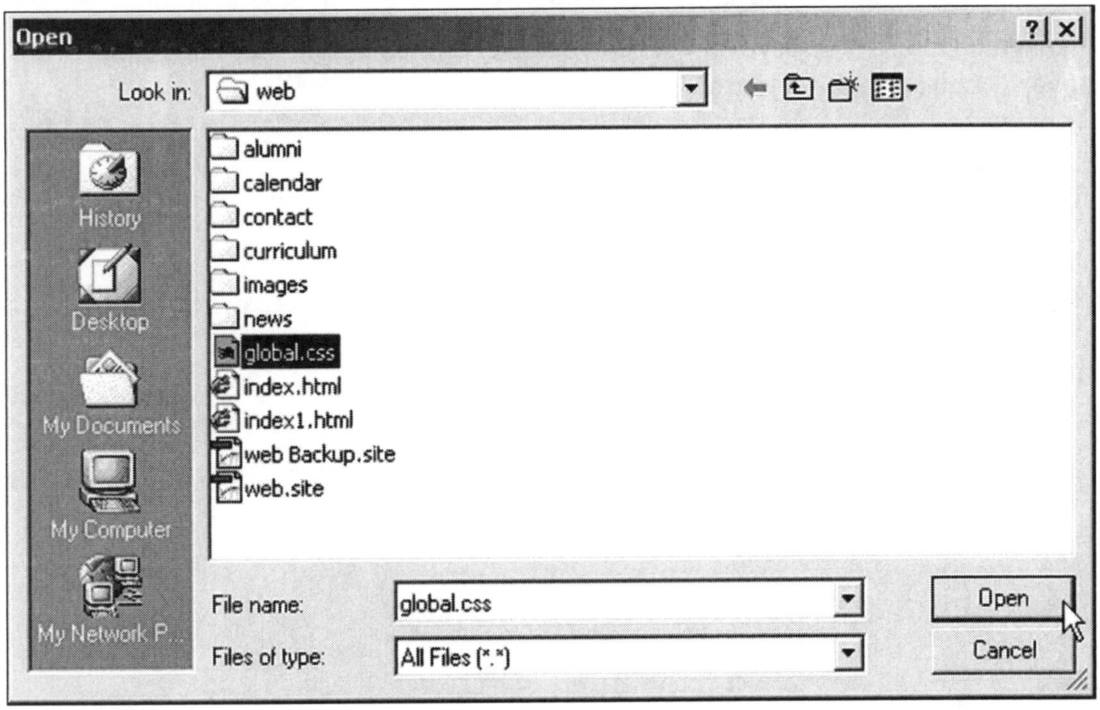

41. The external style sheet global.css has now been linked to index.html.

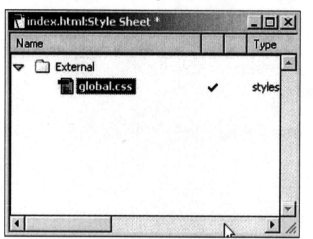

42. Close the style sheet and the index.html window, and save the changes when prompted.

43. Open index1.html and repeat Steps 37 through 42 to link this file to global.css also.

44. Close all windows and save when prompted.

Congratulations! You have now set up your site, created a style sheet, and linked your page templates to this style sheet!

Check Your Understanding

1. The web is a type of media that allows for user interactivity.

    A. True

    B. False

2. What design principle does the use of the same set of buttons on every web page illustrate?

    A. Clarity

    B. Contrast

    C. Consistency

    D. Simplicity

3. Which World Wide Web feature interconnects related web pages?

    A. URL

    B. Mouse pointer

    C. Underlined text

    D. Hypertext

4. How a browser interprets tags affects how a web page appears.

    A. True

    B. False

5. What type of font is Times?

    A. Serif

    B. Sans serif

    C. Display

    D. Italics

6. What is one way to unify and enhance a design?

    A. Make all shapes on the page different in shape and size.

    B. Include numerous fonts.

    C. Use a large palette of colors.

    D. Establish a dominant color theme.

7. What can designers use to control how elements are displayed?

   A. Frames

   B. Content surfacing

   C. Style sheet

   D. Stickiness

8. Both tables and frames can be used to make sections of a web page static.

   A. True

   B. False

9. Why is the W3C presenting CSS as a standard for web use?

   A. Because the newer browsers do not support GIF.

   B. For integration with legacy database systems.

   C. So that designers can control layout.

   D. They are attempting to find another way to show animations on web pages.

10. A table with a set pixel width might look differently on a 640 x 480 monitor than an 800 x 600 monitor.

    A. True

    B. False

11. Which of the following is not an example of emphasis?

    A. Using a large color palette

    B. Centering text

    C. Highlighting text

    D. Using large, bold text

12. Which design principle is illustrated by the use of symbols that are easily understood by the user?

    A. Emphasis

    B. Structure

    C. Consistency

    D. Clarity

13. Style sheets specify how a web page will appear, including fonts, colors, alignment, and other visual elements.

    A. True

    B. False

14. One of the ways to hook users is to have the home page load quickly and properly.

    A. True

    B. False

15. What happens if a font is not installed on the computer displaying the web page?

    A. The font is still displayed.

    B. No text is displayed.

    C. The system uses a default font.

    D. None of the above.

16. Frames enable the web designer to divide the browser display area into sections.

    A. True

    B. False

17. Which markup languages incorporate the separation of structure and content?

    A. XML, DHTML, and XHTML

    B. XML, HTML 4.01, and XHTML

    C. XML and XHTML only

    D. XML only

18. What is the design principle used when large, bold text is placed in the center of a page?

    A. Clarity

    B. Contrast

    C. Emphasis

    D. Structure

19. One reason that W3C is adopting style sheets is so that HTML can be used strictly for structure.

    A. True

    B. False

20. How does a user override the designer's style sheets?

    A. The browser's default will override them anyways.

    B. The user's preference overrides the designer's style sheets.

    C. The user can specify that he/she will not accept external style sheets.

    D. The user cannot override them.

Chapter 6
User Interface Design

Introduction

In this chapter, you investigate several websites and analyze their navigational schemes and usability. In addition, you find examples of page layouts on the web. You can use these examples of page layouts when you are designing your own projects.

The six labs in this chapter show you how to add layout items, create navigation items, and set up the different sections for the course project website. You need to use Adobe GoLive for all six labs.

Focus Questions

1. What are the differences between the dormant and active states of rollover buttons?

2. What is an image table?

3. What is the purpose of the frameset?

4. What is usability? What makes a site more usable than another?

5. What is an intra-page link?

6. What is parallel navigation?

7. What are the advantages of client-side image maps?

8. What is a GUI? What are its components?

_____

_____

_____

_____

9. How could you apply color-coding to your website?

_____

_____

10. What are the three questions that navigation elements should answer?

_____

_____

_____

Discovery Exercises

Learn to Analyze Websites

Go to three of your favorite sites and answer the following questions.

First Site

URL: _____

Is the subject or purpose of the site obvious? _____

Does the color scheme reflect the tone of the company?_____

What do you think about the logo and headers? _____

_____

Is it easy to navigate around the site? _____

Are the navigation elements in the same place on every page? _____

Are navigation elements grouped logically? _____

Is the structure of the site deep or wide? Is it appropriate for the size and scope of the site? _____

_____

How long is the download time of the home page? Typical pages? _____

On a scale of 1 to 10, with 10 being the highest score, what would you rate the usability of this site? _____

Why did you give it this score? What can be improved? _____

_____

_____

Second Site

URL: _____

Is the subject or purpose of the site obvious? _____

Does the color scheme reflect the tone of the company?_____

What do you think about the logo and headers? _____

_____

Is it easy to navigate around the site? _____

Are the navigation elements in the same place on every page? _____

Are navigation elements grouped logically? _____

Is the structure of the site deep or wide? Is it appropriate for the size and scope of the site? _____

_____

How long is the download time of the home page? Typical pages? _____

On a scale of 1 to 10, with 10 being the highest score, what would you rate the usability of this site? _____

Why did you give it this score? What can be improved? _____

_____

_____

Third Site

URL: _____

Is the subject or purpose of the site obvious? _____

Does the color scheme reflect the tone of the company?_____

What do you think about the logo and headers? _____

_____

Is it easy to navigate around the site? _____

Are the navigation elements in the same place on every page? _____

Are navigation elements grouped logically? _____

Is the structure of the site deep or wide? Is it appropriate for the size and scope of the site? _____

_____

How long is the download time of the home page? Typical pages? _____

On a scale of 1 to 10, with 10 being the highest score, what would you rate the usability of this site? _____

Why did you give it this score? What can be improved? _____

_____

_____

Structure

Find five websites with different layouts. Print them out and paste them to the following pages to create a scrapbook of layouts, which you can use when designing a layout for future projects.

First Site Layout

URL: _____

What do you like about this layout? _____

What do you not like about this layout? _____

(Print out and paste the layout in the following space.)

Second Site Layout

URL: _____

What do you like about this layout? _____

What do you not like about this layout? _____

(Print out and paste the layout in the following space.)

Third Site Layout

URL: _____

What do you like about this layout? _____

What do you not like about this layout? _____

(Print out and paste the layout in the following space.)

Fourth Site Layout

URL: _____

What do you like about this layout? _____

What do you not like about this layout? _____

(Print out and paste the layout in the following space.)

Fifth Site Layout

URL: _____

What do you like about this layout? _____

What do you not like about this layout? _____

(Print out and paste the layout in the following space.)

Lab 6.1: Adding Layout Items (GoLive)

In this lab, you integrate the navigation buttons (the normal version) that you created before in your page templates. You also add background colors and create the main section pages.

You can add layout items to a website using several different methods. The steps in this lab are designed for the beginning student who has never used GoLive. As you become more proficient with GoLive, you will devise methods that reduce steps and optimize your time.

1. Open your website in GoLive (select File, Open, and find the web.site file).

2. Double-click index.html to open it. Your fonts are now displayed in Arial and 10pt. This is the style sheet information that is applied though linking the style sheet.

3. From the Objects palette, Basic tab, drag the Image Icon [?] to the Header Cell.

4. Delete the word Header. Select the image icon. In the Inspector window, click the Browse button [] and browse to this path: web/image/header/. Select the header.gif, and click Open.

5. The header image now shows up in your Layout editor of the index.html file.

6. You can now assign the images for the cells that make up the navigation bar by using the same technique as before.

Note: The order of the buttons from left to right is News, Calendar, Curriculum, Alumni, and Contact.

The path to the navigation buttons is web/images/navigation, and the files to select are the ones without any extension (like .dn or .ov) in their filename. For example, choose news.gif, but not newsdn.gif.

After all normal-state navigation buttons have been assigned, your index.html should look like what is shown here.

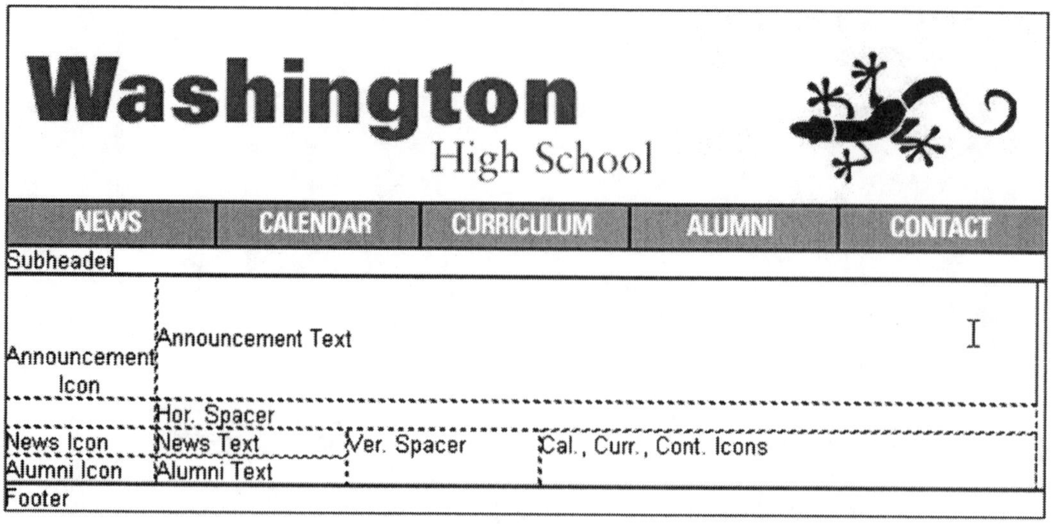

7. Now select the Subheader cell, as shown here.

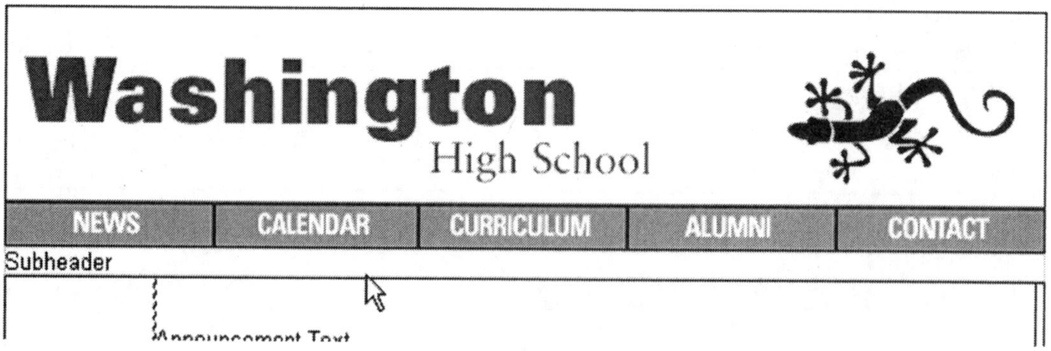

8. In the Inspector window under the Cell Tab, assign a background color to the Subheader cell by clicking the color field box on the right. Then under the Color Tab, enter the RGB value: 51, 102, 153. Drag the color from the color area on the left of the Objects window over to the Color field in the Inspector window:

The result looks like this.

9. Change the page title to Washington High School by typing it into the left-top corner, as shown here.

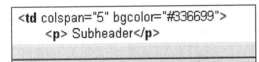

10. Save your file.

11. To assign the style to the Subheader cell's font, place your cursor next to the word Subheader and then select the Source Tab [Source T] in the Editor window. This shows you the HTML code of you index.html file. The cursor automatically returns to exactly the same place that you placed it before in the layout view: It is next to the word Subheader, as shown here.

```
<td colspan="5" bgcolor="#336699">
    <p> Subheader</p>
```

Note: On the Macintosh using GoLive 5.0, the HTML code differs from the image above. It looks like the following:

```
<td colspan="5" bgcolor="#336699">Subheader</td>
```

12. To assign the style, move to the line above the Subheader text. This line is defining the Subheader cell's properties and starts with the <td> tag. To this line, you add the code class="WelcomeHeader" as shown here (note the spaces in front and behind this code).

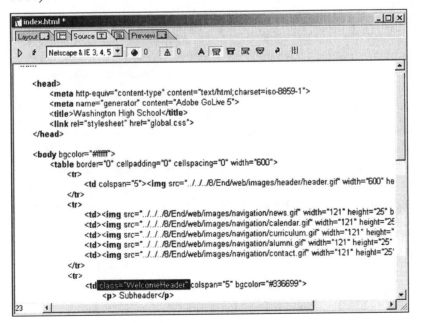

13. After you switch back to Layout view, you can see that the word Subheader is now a light blue-green, bold, and 16pt. Now change the word to read WELCOME LIZARDS!. Your result looks like this.

14. Save your file and close it.

15. Open index1.html.

16. Insert the header image and the navigation buttons as you did before.

17. You can now apply the correct style to the Subheader cell the same way you did before. The only difference is that this time, you will use the code class="Header" because this page template is for all pages other than the home page, and their format is slightly different.

```
<td class="Header" colspan="5">Subheader</td>
```

18. Change the page title to Washington High School by typing it into the top-left corner.

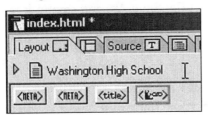

19. Save your file.

20. Because the font color of the Header style is white, you will not see anything when switching back to Layout view until you apply a background color to the cell. Assign the RGB value 255, 102, 0 to this cell as you did before.

Your result looks like this.

21. Now replace the word Subheader with NEWS (note the capitalization).

22. It is time to create actual content pages. To do this, you need to save index1.html (the file that you are presently editing) by choosing File, Save As, and saving it in web/news as main.html, as shown here.

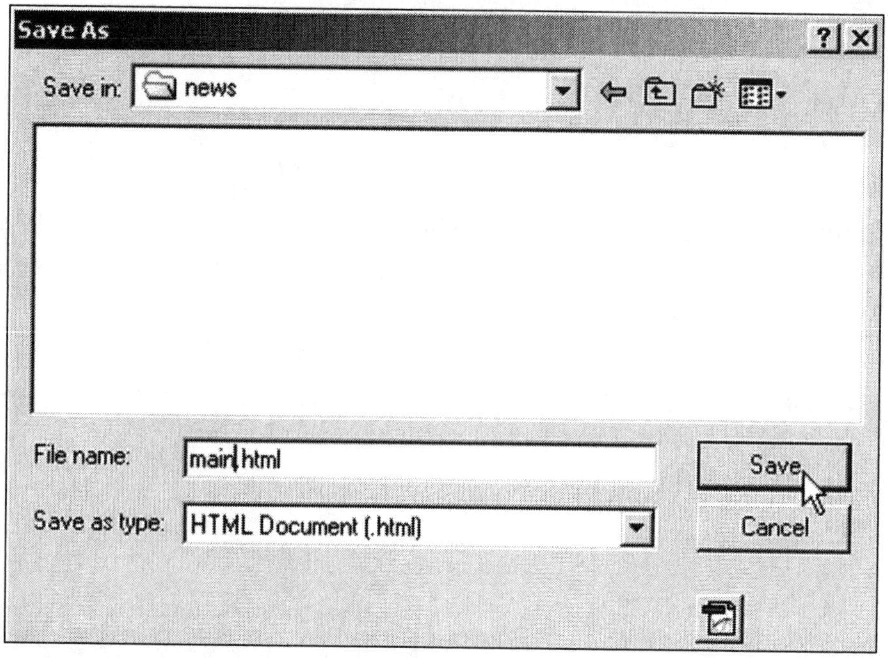

23. Now save this file by choosing File, Save As and saving it in web/calendar as main.html.

24. Change the background color of the Subheader cell to RGB 204,51,0, and change the word NEWS to CALENDAR.

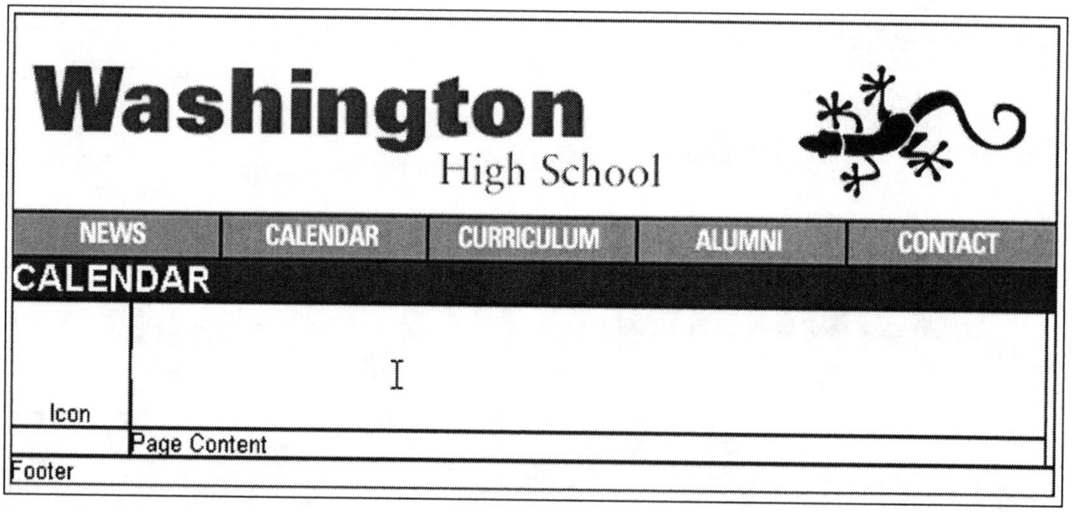

25. Save the file with the new changes. Follow the general structure of Steps 22-24 as you create the remainder of the content pages.

26. You need to generate the main.html in the web/curriculum folder, assign the background color of the Subheader cell to RGB 153,0,102, and change the word to CURRICULUM.

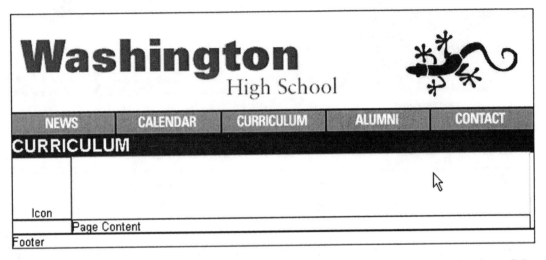

27. Generate the main.html for the web/alumni folder, assign the background color of the Subheader cell to RGB 0,102,102, and change the word to ALUMNI.

28. Finally, generate the main.html for the web/contact folder, assign the background color of the Subheader cell to RGB 102,102,0, and change the word to CONTACT.

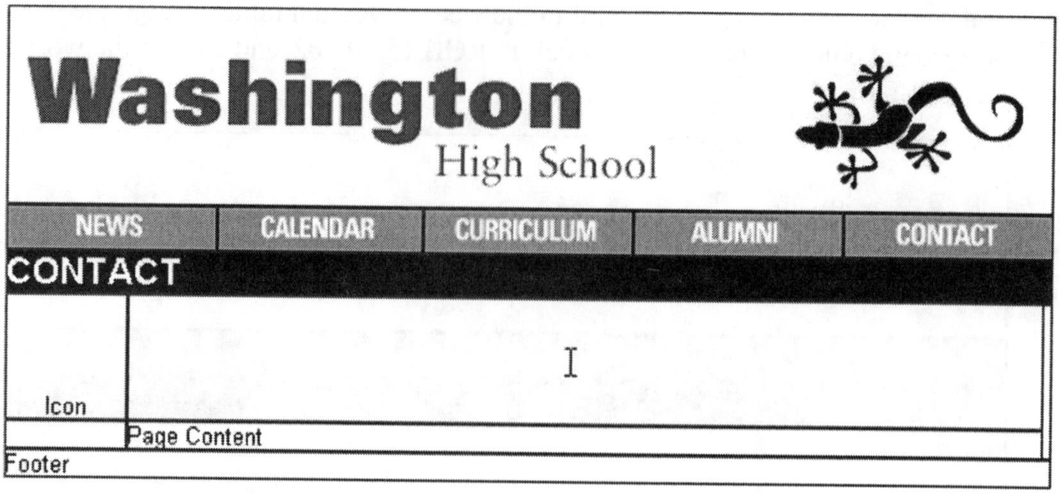

29. With that, you have generated the home page and the main section pages for your website and integrated the main design elements. Save all your files.

Note: On the Mac, the web Backup.site and web.site files are not displayed in the window. Instead, they can be viewed on the desktop in the web folder. Also, the file icons for the .html files have a GoLive icon as opposed to the Internet Explorer icons, as shown here.

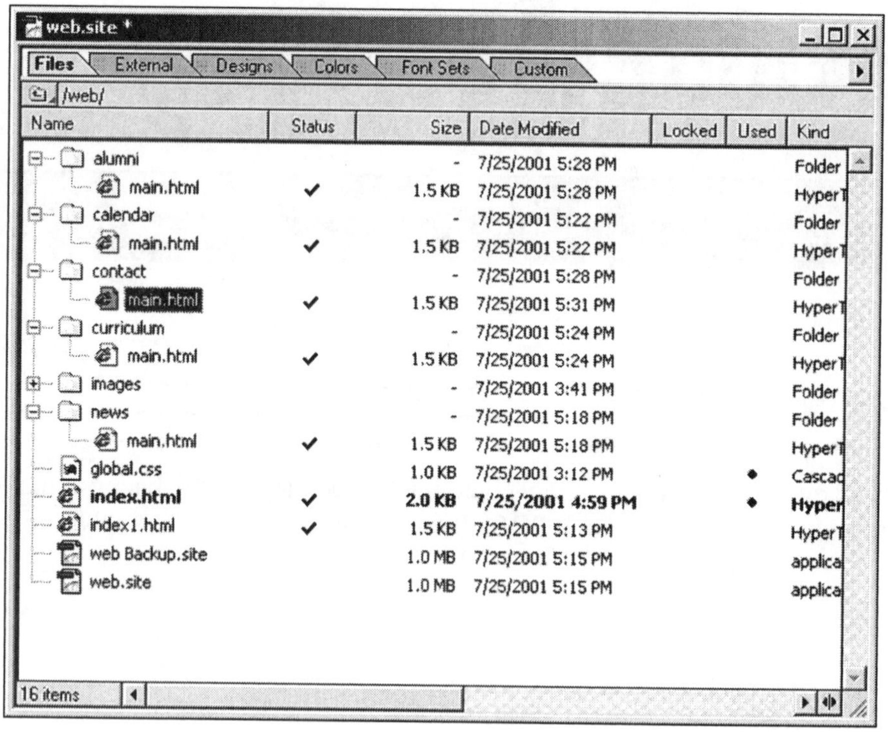

Lab 6.2: Creating the Navigation Items (GoLive)

In Lab 6.1, you set up the static navigation bar and created the main section pages in their respective folders.

Now, you are ready to set up all the navigation items and make them functional by adding JavaScript and links.Start Adobe GoLive, and open your website.

1. Open the file index.html.

2. Start assigning links to the navigation buttons. Select the News button and note the change in the Image Inspector.

3. In the Image Inspector under the Basic Tab, enter the word News in the Alt Text field.

4. Switch to the Link Tab, and click the Assign Link button ⬚ .

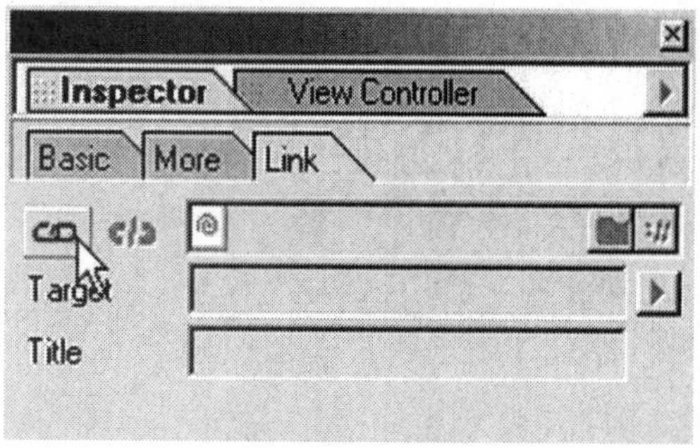

5. In the field to the right of the Assign Link button, (Empty Reference!) appears. To assign a reference (= link), click the Browse button (the file folder icon).

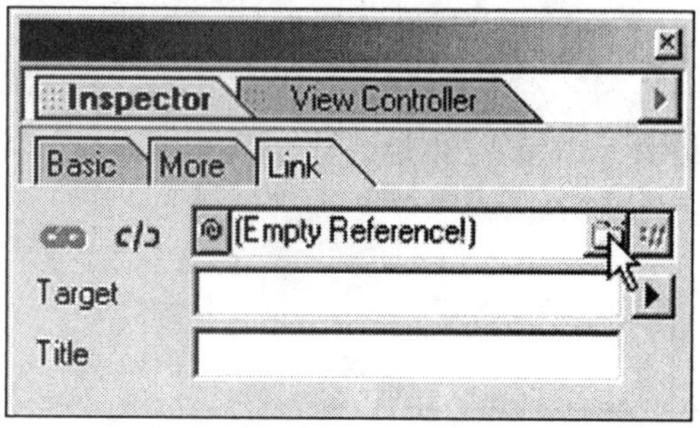

6. Browse to the main.html file in the news folder (web/news/main.html), and click Open to assign the link, as shown here.

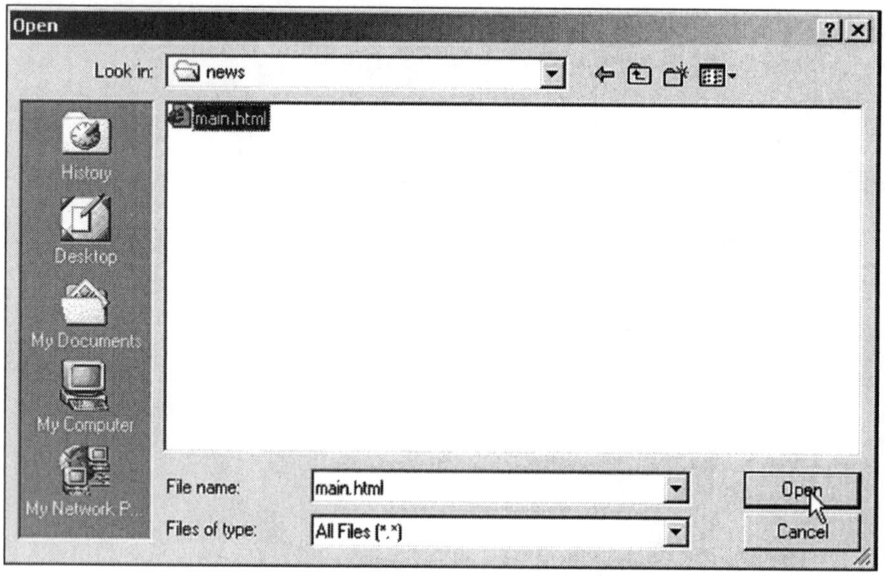

7. The result looks like what is shown here.

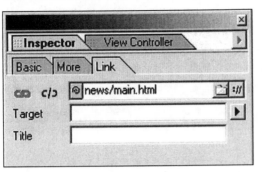

8. Assign a link and the Alt Text to the Calendar button by selecting the button in the Image Inspector, clicking the Assign Link button and browsing to the file web/calendar/main.html.

9. Now assign links and the Alt Text to the Curriculum (web/curriculum/main.html), Alumni (web/alumni/main.html) and Contact (web/contact/main.html) buttons by repeating Step 8 for each.

10. Save your file.

11. Place your cursor in the Footer cell at the bottom of the page, delete the word Footer and add the text that will be used as the additional footer navigation bar. Format the text to look like this:

NEWS | CALENDAR | CURRICULUM | ALUMNI | CONTACT

12. Center this cell content by clicking the Align Center button on the top of the application window.

13. Your result will look like this.

14. To link the words in the footer, highlight the word.

15. In the Text Inspector, click the Assign Link button and browse to the correct file. In this case, it is web/news/main.html.

16. Repeat Steps 14 and 15 for each item in the footer. With that, you have completed the footer navigation bar and your result should look like what is shown here.

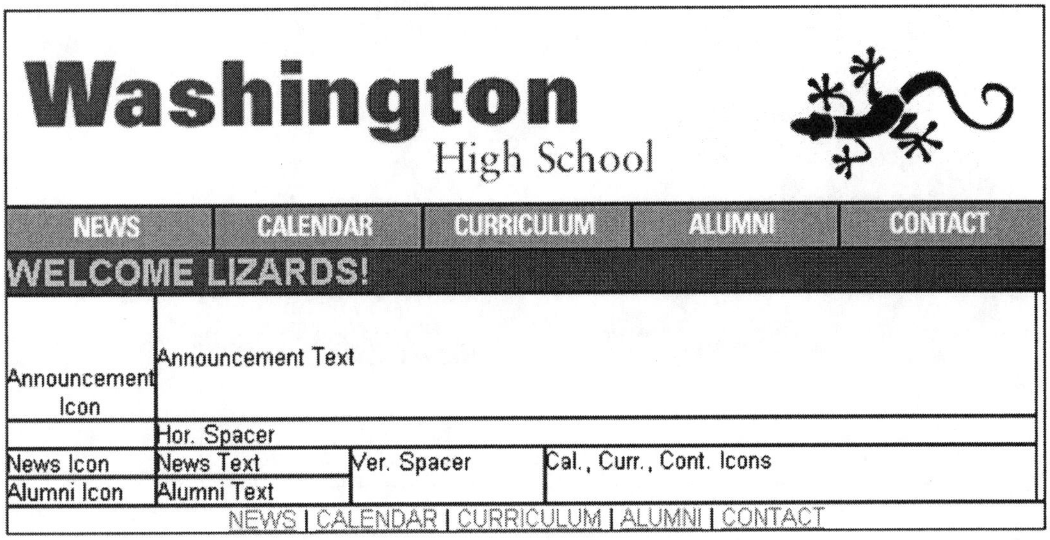

17. Finally, select the header image. In the Image Inspector on the Basic Tab, insert the Alt Text Home. Click the Link Tab and browse to assign a link to web/index.html. This might seem redundant because you are linking to the page that you are already viewing, but it is advisable to do so for consistency so that all other pages will have the same link.

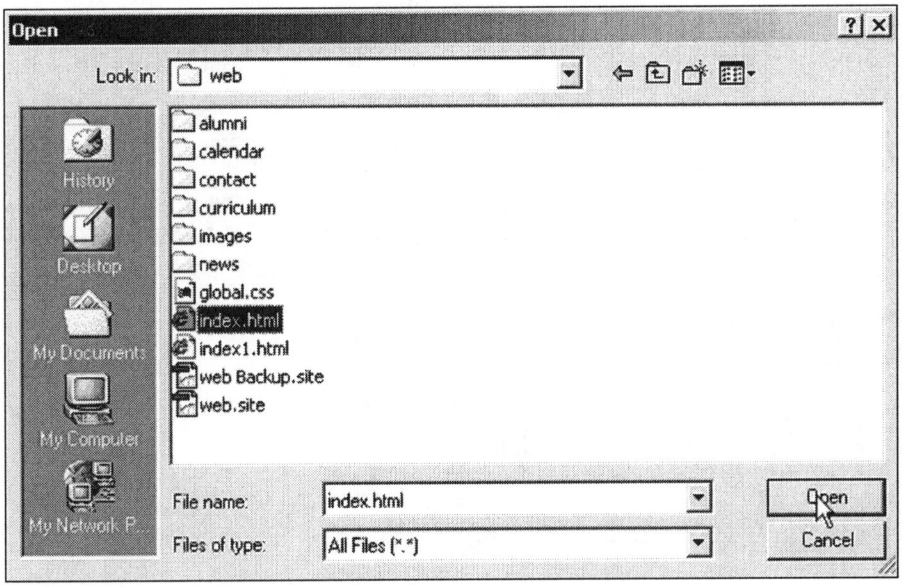

18. Save your file.

Linking the Navigation Buttons

You now need to link the navigation buttons in all main section pages. To do this, follow these steps:

1. Start by opening alumni/main.html.

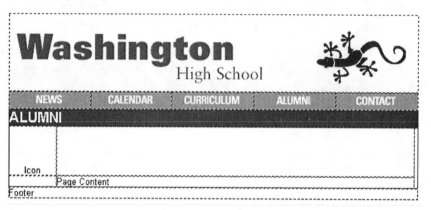

2. Work your way through the navigation buttons, insert the respective Alt Text, and assign the correct link. Here is a list of items that will need to be linked:

    *   News button: web/news/main.html

    *   Calendar button: web/calendar /main.html

    *   Curriculum button: web/curriculum /main.html

    *   Alumni button: web/alumni /main.html

    *   Contact button: web/contact /main.html

3. After you are done, you can switch to the Preview view Preview and check the links by placing the mouse over each link and making sure it turns into a hand. Also, if you are a PC user, take a look at the status bar at the bottom of this window, which shows you the linking path.

4. Now you can assign the Alt Text, and the link to the header image. (*Remember*: The link will point to web/index.html, as shown here).

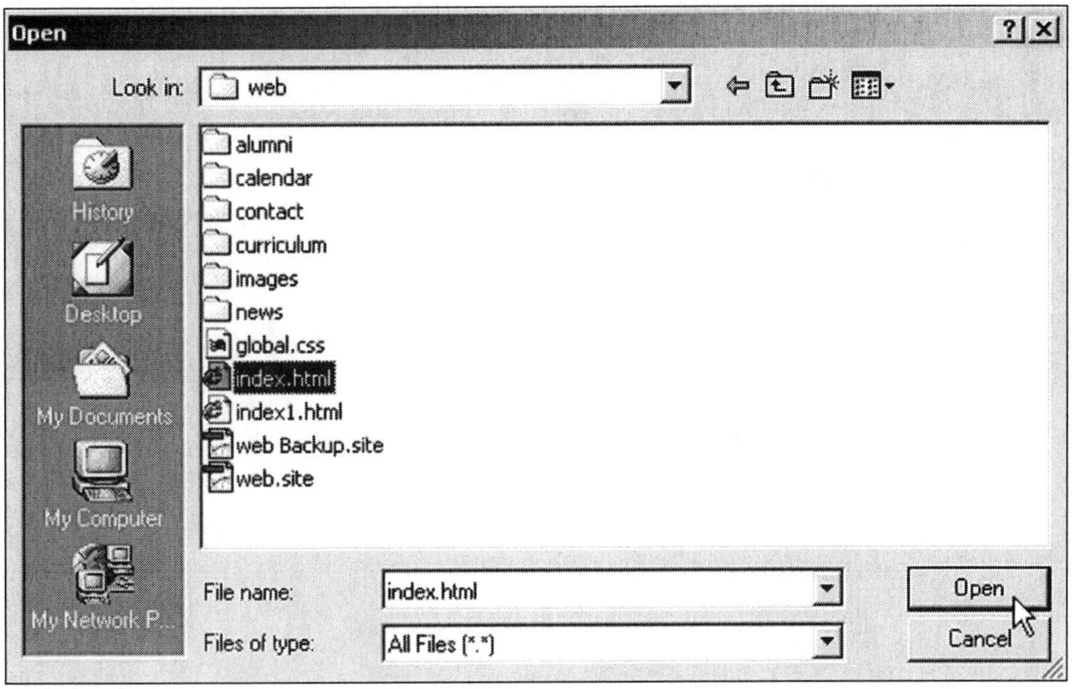

5. You can now create the footer menu bar like you did in Steps 11 through 16 in the previous section of the lab. Test your result in the Preview window. If you are using a PC, can you see the hover effect (for example, when you place your mouse over the text, it gets lighter) on your text links in the footer navigation bar? This is caused by the style sheet that you created earlier. This hover effect does not work in preview mode for Mac users.

6. Save this as index1.html.

7. Repeat these steps for each main.html. This is a list for you to work through.

   Calendar/main.html:

   - Insert five Alt Texts for the navigation buttons.

   - Assign five links to the navigation bar buttons.

   - Create the footer navigation bar text (five words).

   - Assign the links to the footer navigation bar text (five links).

   - Insert the Alt Text to the header image.

   - Link the header image to the home page.

Add JavaScript Code

8. To set up the rollovers for your navigation bar, you need to use JavaScript. The JavaScript code that follows can be copied from the companion CD and pasted into index.html, or you can type the code (Make sure you type the code properly). If you

want to copy the script, make sure the companion CD is in the CD-ROM drive. Double-click the javascript_filename. Highlight all the text and press Ctrl--C (PC) or Command-C (Mac) to copy the code.

Note

It is a common practice in web development to take free template scripts or code that is available from websites and modify the code. Sometimes, the website requires you to attribute them in the source code, which you should so when requested. This particular code does not require any references.

```
if (document.images) {
  b1on = new Image();
  b1on.src = "images/navigation/newsov.gif";
  b2on = new Image();
  b2on.src = "images/navigation/calendarov.gif";
  b3on = new Image();
  b3on.src = "images/navigation/curriculumov.gif";
  b4on = new Image();
  b4on.src = "images/navigation/alumniov.gif";
  b5on = new Image();
  b5on.src = "images/navigation/contactov.gif";
  b1off = new Image();
  b1off.src = "images/navigation/news.gif";
  b2off = new Image();
  b2off.src = "images/navigation/calendar.gif";
  b3off = new Image();
  b3off.src = "images/navigation/curriculum.gif";
  b4off = new Image();
  b4off.src = "images/navigation/alumni.gif";
  b5off = new Image();
  b5off.src = "images/navigation/contact.gif";
  b1dn = new Image();
  b1dn.src = "images/navigation/newsdn.gif";
  b2dn = new Image();
  b2dn.src = "images/navigation/calendardn.gif";
  b3dn = new Image();
  b3dn.src = "images/navigation/curriculumdn.gif";
  b4dn = new Image();
  b4dn.src = "images/navigation/alumnidn.gif";
  b5dn = new Image();
```

```
    b5dn.src = "images/navigation/contactdn.gif";
  }


function changeImages() {
  if (document.images) {
    for (var i=0; i<changeImages.arguments.length; i+=2) {
      document[changeImages.arguments[i]].src =
eval(changeImages.arguments[i+1] + ".src");
    }
  }
}
```

---

9. After copying the code, you need to paste it into index.html by clicking the Scripts Window button 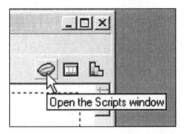 in the Layout window.

10. In the Scripts window, click the Create script button.

11. Right-click to bring up the context menu and select Paste. If you did not use the same filenaming convention as suggested for the images created in previous labs, you need to change the filenames (or folder references) within the JavaScript to match yours exactly after you have pasted the code.

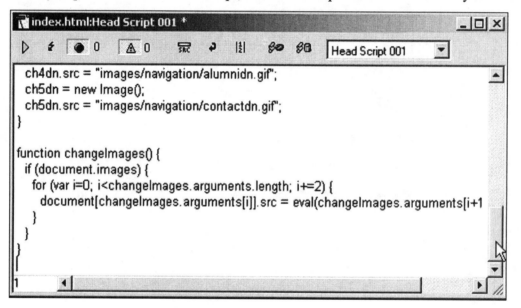

12. After you paste and review the script, close the Scripts window and save your file.

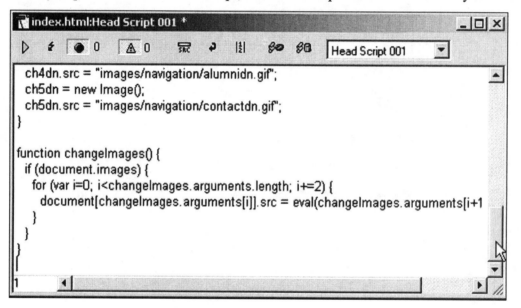

13. Switch from the Layout view to the Source Code view, and scroll to the top where <script> indicates the start of the JavaScript section.

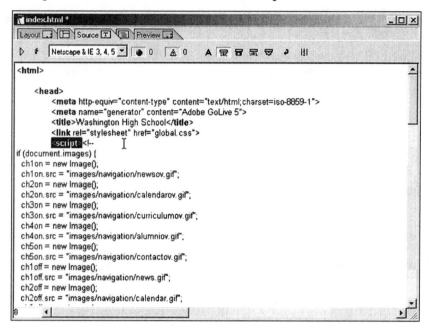

Add a Language Identifier

14. Place your cursor between "<script" and ">" and type this string: language="JavaScript" to indicate what type of script you just inserted. The script tags now should read: <script language="JavaScript">.

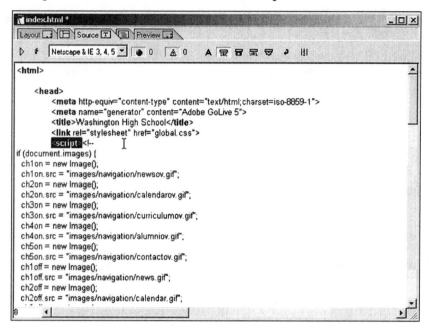

15. Switch back to Layout view and note that the Script Icon now appears in the header area of your Layout view because you added a script to this file.

16. Save your file.

17. The next step is setting up MouseOver, MouseOut, MouseDown, and MouseUp events for each navigation button. Do this by using the Source View window, because this will be easier and faster than using GoLive's Action window.
    The Mouse events together with the JavaScript that you just inserted will react to your mouse actions and will trigger the different button image states to be displayed whenever the mouse is placed over a button (MouseOver), whenever the mouse exits a button (MouseOut), whenever the left mouse button is held down (MouseDown), and whenever the left mouse button is released (MouseUp).

18. Now insert the code necessary to trigger the Mouse events. Start by switching to the Source View and scroll to the code that defines the navigation bar images (below the body tag).

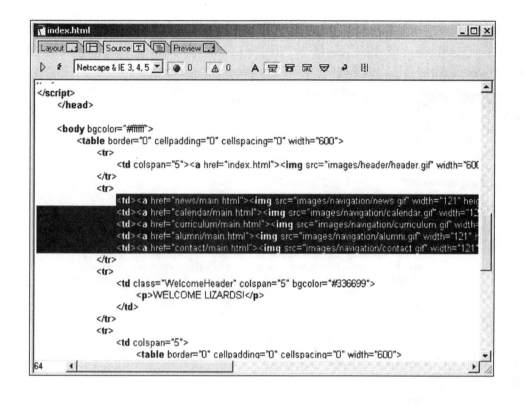

Note

This lab uses all the navigation button states that you created earlier. You can find them in the web/images/navigation folder, as shown here.

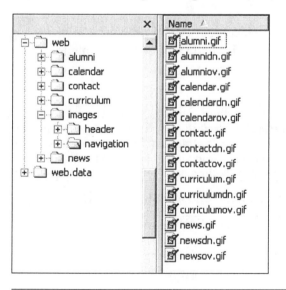

---

19. Switch on the Row Number in the Source View window by clicking the Row Number button ⊞ at the top of the window. You can use these row numbers to quickly find lines of code. *Note*: The numbers in the figures might not match yours.

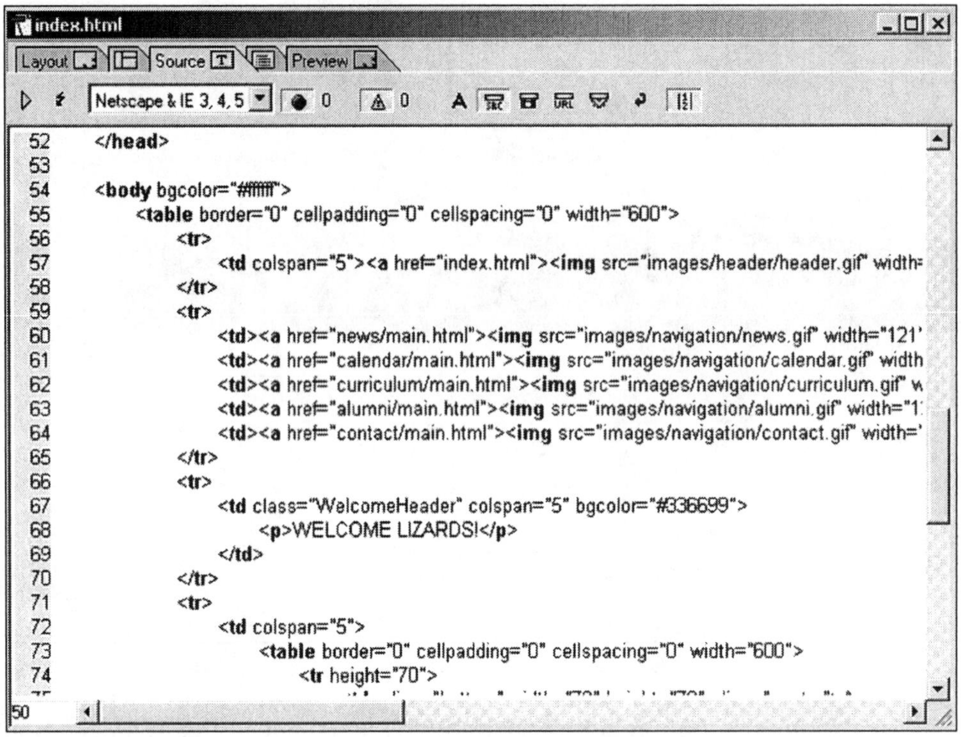

Name Image Tags

20. Start with the first cell in the second row. Place your cursor between the image tag (<img) and the src attribute. The name-identifier code will communicate to the JavaScript code which particular image state needs to appear with which event. Add a name to this image: name="b1".

21. Add an identifier to each of the other image tags following the specifications.

Website Section	Identifier Code
calendar	name="b2"
curriculum	name="b3"
alumni	name="b4"
contact	name="b5"

```
60   <td><a href="news/main.html"><img name="b1" src="images/navigation/news.gif"
61   <td><a href="calendar/main.html"><img name="b2" src="images/navigation/calen
62   <td><a href="curriculum/main.html"><img name="b3" src="images/navigation/cur
63   <td><a href="alumni/main.html"><img name="b4" src="images/navigation/alumni.
64   <td><a href="contact/main.html"><img name="b5" src="images/navigation/contac
```

22. Save your file.

Create Mouse Events

23. You now need to connect the Mouse events to the link tag (<a>). To do this, place your cursor in the first cell of the second row between the "<a " and "href." Type the following code segment:

```
onMouseOver="changeImages('b1','b1on')"
onMouseDown="changeImages('b1','b1dn')"
onMouseUp="changeImages('b1','b1on')"onMouseOut="changeImages('b1','b1off')"
```

Although this code appears here in four separate lines in your Source window, it should be on just one line. If it is not, please delete the line breaks. Your result should look like this.

```
60 <td><a onMouseOver="changeImages('b1','b1on')" onMouseDown="changeImages('b1','b1dn')
61 <td><a href="calendar/main.html"><img name="b2" src="images/navigation/calendar.gif" widt
62 <td><a href="curriculum/main.html"><img name="b3" src="images/navigation/curriculum.gif"
63 <td><a href="alumni/main.html"><img name="b4" src="images/navigation/alumni.gif" width="
64 <td><a href="contact/main.html"><img name="b5" src="images/navigation/contact.gif" width=
```

24. Make sure to copy the code exactly and double-check it with the code shown in the example. The exact naming and numbering of the image events is crucial to make the navigation bar work the way it is supposed to. Pay special attention to lowercase versus uppercase letters and to single quotes versus double quotes.

25. Now insert the code for the rest of the navigation image links. You can copy and paste the code you just entered. Use this table to make the required changes:

Website Section	Code Segment

Calendar	```onMouseOver="changeImages('b2','b2on')"```
	```onMouseDown="changeImages('b2','b2dn')"```
	```onMouseUp="changeImages('b2','b2on')"```
	```onMouseOut="changeImages('b2','b2off')"```

Curriculum	```onMouseOver="changeImages('b3','b3on')"```
	```onMouseDown="changeImages('b3','b3dn')"```
	```onMouseUp="changeImages('b3','b3on')"```
	```onMouseOut="changeImages('b3','b3off')"```

Alumni	```onMouseOver="changeImages('b4','b4on')"```
	```onMouseDown="changeImages('b4','b4dn')"```
	```onMouseUp="changeImages('b4','b4on')"```
	```onMouseOut="changeImages('b4','b4off')"```

Contact	```onMouseOver="changeImages('b5','b5on')"```
	```onMouseDown="changeImages('b5','b5dn')"```
	```onMouseUp="changeImages('b5','b5on')"```
	```onMouseOut="changeImages('b5','b5off')"```

26. Your result will look like this. *Note*: The code is cut off on the right-hand side:

```
60 <td><a onMouseOver="changeImages('b1','b1on')" onMouseDown="changeImages('b1','b1dn')
61 <td><a onMouseOver="changeImages('b2','b2on')" onMouseDown="changeImages('b2','b2dn')
62 <td><a onMouseOver="changeImages('b3','b3on')" onMouseDown="changeImages('b3','b3dn')
63 <td><a onMouseOver="changeImages('b4','b4on')" onMouseDown="changeImages('b4','b4dn')
64 <td><a onMouseOver="changeImages('b5','b5on')" onMouseDown="changeImages('b5','b5dn')
```

27. Note that there is a space between the "<a" and "onMouseOver...". Make sure that your code looks the same. Check also that there is a space before the href=....

```
60 angeImages('b1','b1on')" onMouseOut="changeImages('b1','b1off')" href="news/main.html"><im
61 angeImages('b2','b2on')" onMouseOut="changeImages('b2','b2off')" href="calendar/main.html"><
62 angeImages('b3','b3on')" onMouseOut="changeImages('b3','b3off')" href="curriculum/main.html">
63 angeImages('b4','b4on')" onMouseOut="changeImages('b4','b4off')" href="alumni/main.html"><in
64 angeImages('b5','b5on')" onMouseOut="changeImages('b5','b5off')" href="contact/main.html"><i
```

28. Save your file with the Save As option:

Testing Navigation

29. Under Edit, Preferences, click the Browsers button 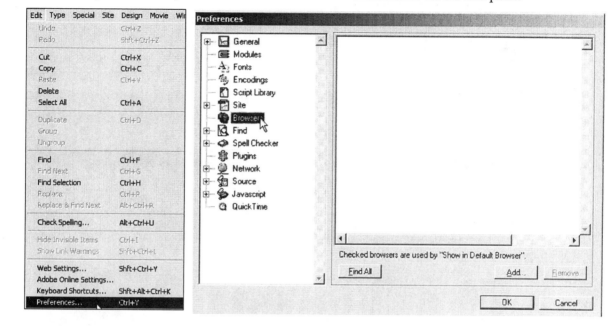 on the left pane.

30. Click the Find All button and wait for GoLive to find an installed browser. Once done, select your default Preview Browser by checking the box in front of it. Please use either Internet Explorer 4.x or Netscape Navigator 4.x. Then click OK:

31. Notice that on the top of your application window, the browser icon appears. Click this icon to display index.html in the browser.

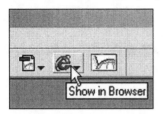

32. Test your rollovers by moving the mouse over each button. You should see the color change for each in addition to seeing the filename for the link in the browser status bar (lower-left corner of the browser window).

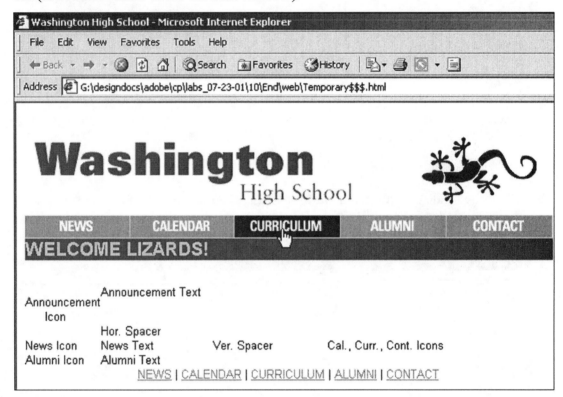

33. If you encounter problems and the button color does not change when you place your mouse over a navigation button, go back and check every step and proofread the code very thoroughly starting from the section, "Add JavaScript Code."

34. If you have an error in your JavaScript, you will get an indication of the line in which the error occurs. Go back to Source View. Switch on the Row Number in the Source View window by clicking the Row Number button () on the top of the window. Look for the line with the error and make the correction. Save your document and preview it again.

35. If everything works, Congratulations!

36. Now you can apply the same principles to the five main section pages. Apply everything starting from the section, "Add JavaScript Code."

Here is a brief overview on the steps you will take:

a) Insert the JavaScript code in the HTML header section ("Add JavaScript Code").

b) Add the language identifier to the script tag (Add Language Identifier).

c) Add the name to the navigation button image tags (Name Image Tags).

d) Add mouse events to the navigation button link tags (Create Mouse Events).

Note

Use the following code for the main section pages instead of the code in the section, "Add JavaScript Code." Because the main.html files are no longer in the root directory of your site but in a subdirectory, the image paths used in the script have changed:

```
if (document.images) {
  b1on = new Image();
  b1on.src = "../images/navigation/newsov.gif";
  b2on = new Image();
  b2on.src = "../images/navigation/calendarov.gif";
  b3on = new Image();
  b3on.src = "../images/navigation/curriculumov.gif";
  b4on = new Image();
  b4on.src = "../images/navigation/alumniov.gif";
  b5on = new Image();
  b5on.src = "../images/navigation/contactov.gif";
  b1off = new Image();
  b1off.src = "../images/navigation/news.gif";
  b2off = new Image();
  b2off.src = "../images/navigation/calendar.gif";
  b3off = new Image();
  b3off.src = "../images/navigation/curriculum.gif";
  b4off = new Image();
  b4off.src = "../images/navigation/alumni.gif";
  b5off = new Image();
  b5off.src = "../images/navigation/contact.gif";
  b1dn = new Image();
  b1dn.src = "../images/navigation/newsdn.gif";
  b2dn = new Image();
  b2dn.src = "../images/navigation/calendardn.gif";
```

Continues

```
  b3dn = new Image();

  b3dn.src = "../images/navigation/curriculumdn.gif";

  b4dn = new Image();

  b4dn.src = "../images/navigation/alumnidn.gif";

  b5dn = new Image();

  b5dn.src = "../images/navigation/contactdn.gif";

}


function changeImages() {

  if (document.images) {

    for (var i=0; i<changeImages.arguments.length; i+=2) {

      document[changeImages.arguments[i]].src =
eval(changeImages.arguments[i+1] + ".src");

    }

  }

}
```

---

37. Test the files in your browser via the Show in Browser button in GoLive. You can also test your site by opening a browser and then open your site by navigating to web/index.html. Because the home and the main section pages have been set up, you are now able to navigate around the site and test the links and rollovers.

Lab 6.3: Setting Up the News Section Pages (GoLive)

Now that you have prepared the navigation items and also added the standard layout items to your home and main section pages, it is time to create the subsection pages. These will be created per section, and you will start with the news section. After that, you also add content to these pages, and complete the News Section setup.

In this lab, you insert content assets like icons and text. These assets have been created for you on the CD and are now available in your web or assets folder. You can copy the icons folder into the website to make them easily available.

1. Start with opening your site in GoLive.

2. Open the web.site window in GoLive.

3. In the web.site window, double-click news/main.html to open the file.

4. Switch to the layout view.

5. You will start by inserting the icon image to the Icon Cell on the left hand side beneath the navigation bar. To do this, delete the word Icon, and from the Object palette, Basic tab, drag over the Image Icon to the Icon Cell.

6. In the Image Inspector, add News Icon as Alt Text (a). Then assign an image file by clicking the browse button ⬚ and browse to web/images/icons/ newsicon.gif (b,c).

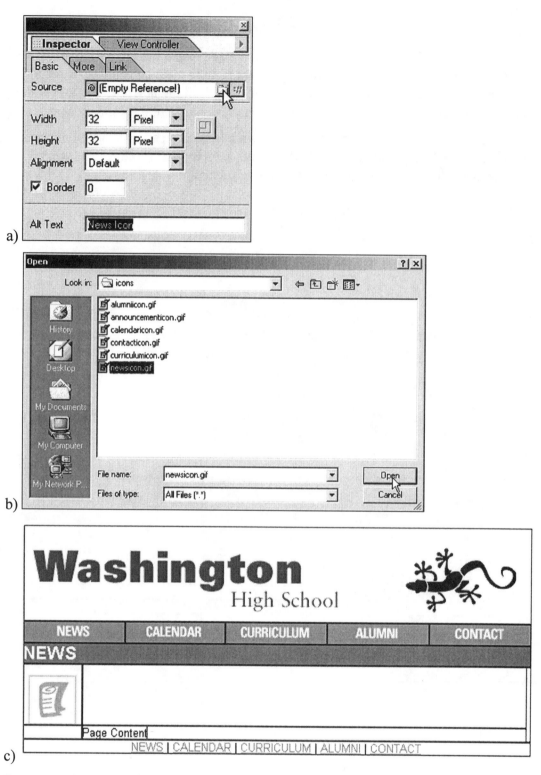

a)

b)

c)

7. Save your file.

8. Create the subsection pages for your news section by saving main.html as current.html, archive1.html, and archive2.html in your web/news directory, as shown here.

9. In the GoLive site window, the result looks like this.

Main Page Content

10. Close the archive2.html window, and open news/main.html again.

11. By using your File Explorer, go to assets/news and open Main.doc. This file contains the text assets for your main news page. Select all the text, copy it, and switch back to GoLive. Replace the words Page Content with the text in your clipboard by pasting it, as shown here.

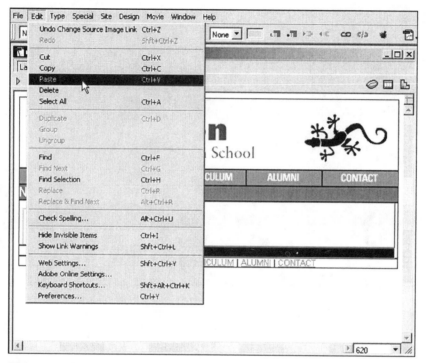

12. Your result will look like this.

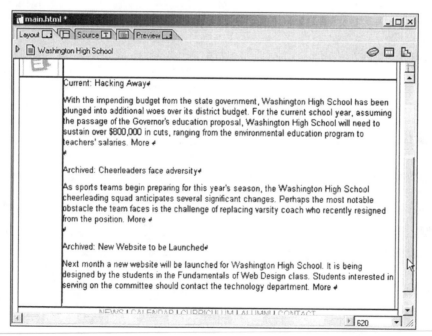

13. Now create a horizontal spacer by dragging the Line Icon ⬓ from the Objects palette to the page content cell and placing it right before the first word in this cell, Current.

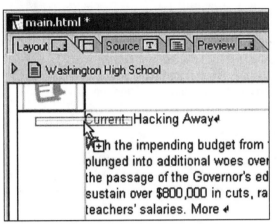

14. Apply a Header 2 Style to the title Current: Hacking Away by selecting these words and right-clicking (PC) or control-clicking (Mac) them. In the Context menu, choose Header, Header 2.

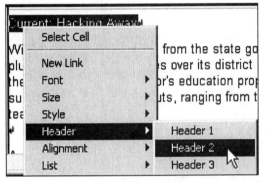

15. You can now delete the line break indicated by the arrow (↵) behind this title.

16. Save your file.

17. Apply the Header 2 Style to the other two titles and delete all remaining line breaks. Your result looks like this.

Current: Hacking Away

With the impending budget from the state government, Washington High School has been plunged into additional woes over its district budget. For the current school year, assuming the passage of the Governor's education proposal, Washington High School will need to sustain over $800,000 in cuts, ranging from the environmental education program to teachers' salaries. More

Archived: Cheerleaders face adversity

As sports teams begin preparing for this year's season, the Washington High School cheerleading squad anticipates several significant changes. Perhaps the most notable obstacle the team faces is the challenge of replacing varsity coach who recently resigned from the position. More

Archived: New Website to be Launched

Next month a new website will be launched for Washington High School. It is being designed by the students in the Fundamentals of Web Design class. Students interested in serving on the committee should contact the technology department. More

18. Link the article leads (the first paragraphs of the articles) to the pages that contain the full article. Do this by linking the article titles and the word More at the end of each lead paragraph. Start by selecting the words Hacking Away in the first title, and click the Link icon in the Text Inspector.

Current: Hacking Away

With the impending budget from t
plunged into additional woes over
the passage of the Governor's edu
sustain over $800,000 in cuts, rar
teachers' salaries. More

Archived: Cheerleaders f

19. Assign a link to the web/news/current.html file.

20. Save the file, and test the result in your browser by opening your site (open web/index.html) and navigating to the news section. Note that the status bar at the bottom shows you where the link points.

21. Assign the same link to the word More at the end of the first paragraph.

22. Now assign links to the two remaining titles and two More words. Use this list to help you:

- "Cheerleaders face adversity", "More" link to archive1.html.

- "New Website to be Launched", More link to archive2.html.

23. Save your file, and test your results in the browser. You might need to refresh the browser window.

Current: Hacking Away

With the impending budget from the state government, Washington High School has been plunged into additional woes over its district budget. For the current school year, assuming the passage of the Governor's education proposal, Washington High School will need to sustain over $800,000 in cuts, ranging from the environmental education program to teachers' salaries. More

Archived: Cheerleaders face adversity

As sports teams begin preparing for this year's season, the Washington High School cheerleading squad anticipates several significant changes. Perhaps the most notable obstacle the team faces is the challenge of replacing varsity coach who recently resigned from the position. More

Archived: New Website to be Launched

Next month a new website will be launched for Washington High School. It is being designed by the students in the Fundamentals of Web Design class. Students interested in serving on the committee should contact the technology department. More

Current Page Content

24. Close main.html and open current.html. Also open assets/news/current.doc and copy the complete article into the clipboard. Then switch back to GoLive and paste the text by replacing the words Page Content.

25. Insert the horizontal spacer from the Object palette, Basic Tab by inserting the Line Icon.

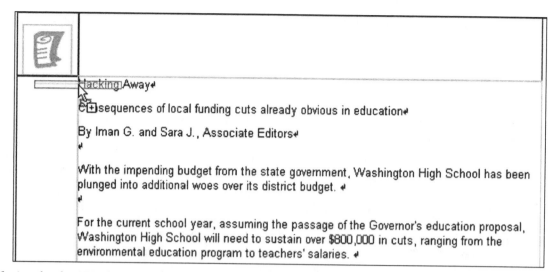

26. Apply the Header 2 Style to the article title, as shown here.

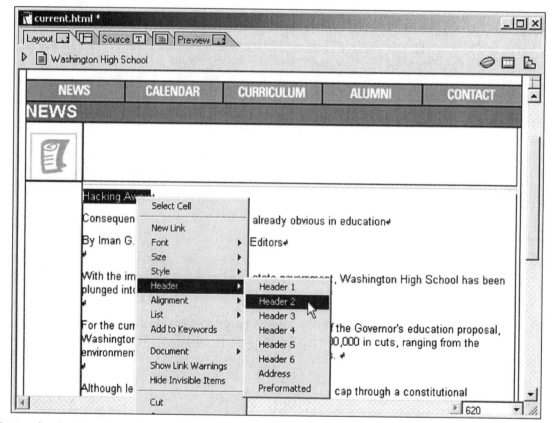

27. Apply the Header 3 Style to the article subtitle (the line that starts with "Consequences...").

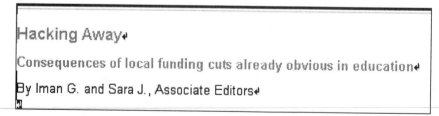

28. Apply the Header 4 Style to the author line (starting with "By…"), and delete the line breaks after the title, subtitle, and author line.

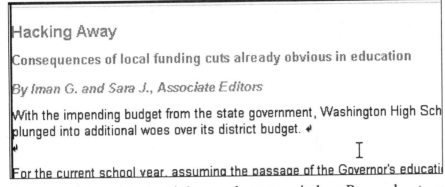

Hacking Away

Consequences of local funding cuts already obvious in education

By Iman G. and Sara J., Associate Editors

With the impending budget from the state government, Washington High Sch plunged into additional woes over its district budget.

For the current school year, assuming the passage of the Governor's educati

29. Save your file and look at it in your browser window. Remember to refresh the browser.

30. To finish the current.html page, you need to add a link back to the main news page. You will do this by adding CURRENT to the word NEWS in the subheader cell:

31. Link the word NEWS to the main.html to provide a means to navigate back to the main news with one click.

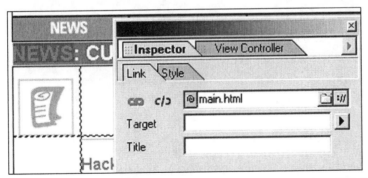

32. After having assigned the link and while NEWS is still highlighted, switch to the Source View and add the class identifier class="h1" `after` the start of the anchor tag (<a) (about line 67).

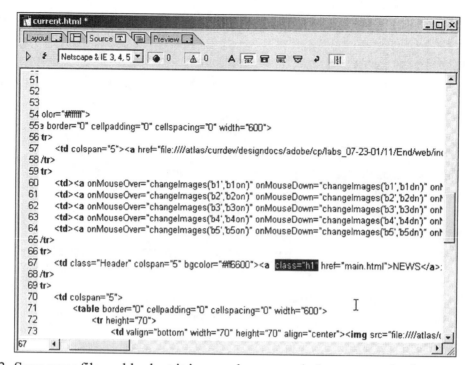

33. Save your file and look at it in your browser window, remembering to refresh the browser.

34. The upper part of your page should look like what's shown here.

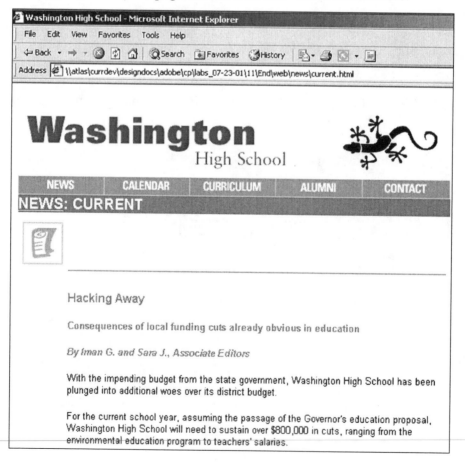

Archive 1: Page Content

35. Close current.html and open archive1.html. Go to the assets/news folder, open archive1.doc, select all text, and copy it to the clipboard.

36. Paste it into the page content cell of archive1.html.

37. Insert the horizontal spacer by inserting the Line Icon from the Objects palette.

38. Scroll to the top and apply the Header Styles to these items:

    a. Article title: Header 2

    b. Article subtitle: Header 3

    c. Article author: Header 4

    Your result should look like what's shown here.

> Cheerleaders face adversity
>
> Changes raise hopes for fewer difficulties in upcoming season
>
> By Tamara O., Web Manager

39. Delete the line breaks behind the title, subtitle, and author lines.

> Cheerleaders face adversity
>
> Changes raise hopes for fewer difficulties in upcoming season
>
> By Tamara O., Web Manager
>
> As sports teams begin preparing for this year's season, the Washington

40. Add the news link to the subheader cell by adding ARCHIVE and linking the word NEWS to main.html.

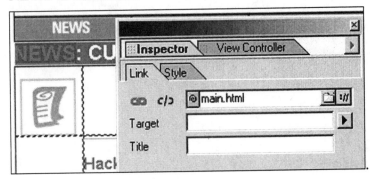

41. After assigning the link and while NEWS is still highlighted, switch to the Source View and add the class identifier, class="h1", behind the start of the anchor tag (<a) (about line number 67).

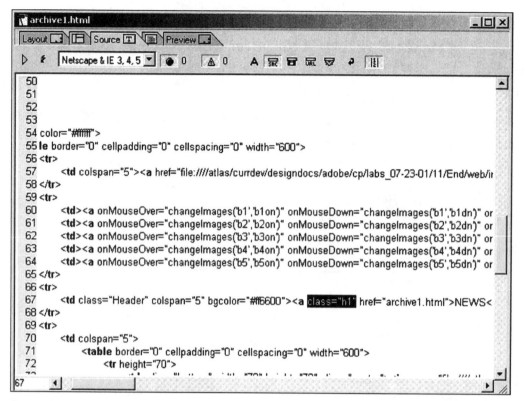

42. Save your file and look at it in your browser window. Remember to refresh the browser.

43. The upper part of your page should look like this.

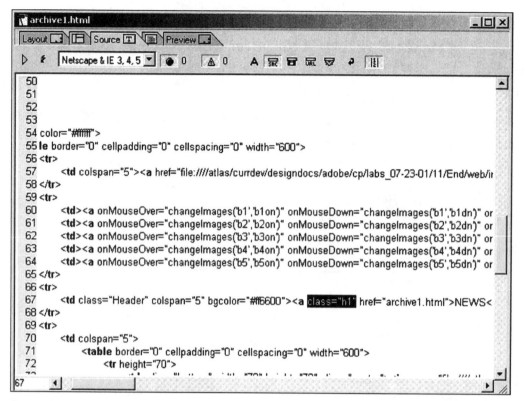

Archive 2: Page Content

44. Close archive1.html and open archive2.html. Go to the Assets folder, open archive2.doc, select all text, and copy it to the clipboard.

45. In GoLive, paste it into the page content cell of archive2.html.

46. Insert the horizontal spacer by inserting the Line icon from the Objects palette.

47. Scroll to the top and apply the Header Styles to these items:

   - Article title: Header 2

   - Article author: Header 4

48. Delete the line breaks behind the title and author lines.

> New Website to be Launched
>
> *By Rashed J. and Gupta R.*
>
> Next month, a new website will be launched

49. Add the news link to the subheader cell by adding the word ARCHIVE and linking the word NEWS to main.html.

50. After having assigned the link and while NEWS is still highlighted, switch to the Source view and add the class identifier "class="h1" behind the start of the "a" tag (about line number 67) as you did before.

51. Save your file, and look at it in your browser window, remembering to refresh the browser.

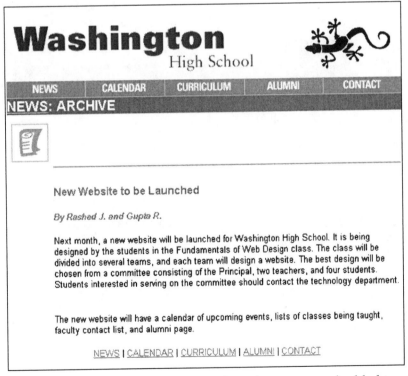

You have now created the news subsection pages and added content to them.

Lab 6.4: Setting Up the Calendar Section Pages (GoLive)

Now that you have set up the news section pages, it is time to create the calendar subsection pages and then add content to these pages. At the end of this lab, you will complete the Calendar section. In this lab, you insert content assets like icons and text. These assets have been created for you, and are now available in your web or assets folder.

Now that you have set up the news section pages, it is time to create the calendar subsection pages and also add content to these pages. At the end of this lab, you will complete the Calendar section of the website. The Calendar section gives web users information about upcoming events taking place at Washington High School.

In this lab, you insert content assets like icons and text. These assets have been created for you, and are now available in your web or assets folder.

1. Start by opening your web.site file in GoLive.

2. Double-click calendar/main.html in the web.site window to open the file.

3. Switch to the Layout view.

4. Start by inserting the Image icon in the Icon cell on the left-hand side beneath the navigation bar. To do this, delete the word Icon, and from the Object palette, Basic tab, drag over the Image Icon to the Icon Cell.

5. Select the Image icon. In the Image Inspector, add Calendar Icon as Alt Text (a) and then assign an image file by clicking the browse button ⬜ and browse to web/images/icons/calendaricon.gif (b).

a)

b)

6. Save your file.

7. Create the subsection pages for your Calendar section by saving the main.html as school.html and athletic.html in your web/calendar directory.

8. In the GoLive site window, the result looks like this.

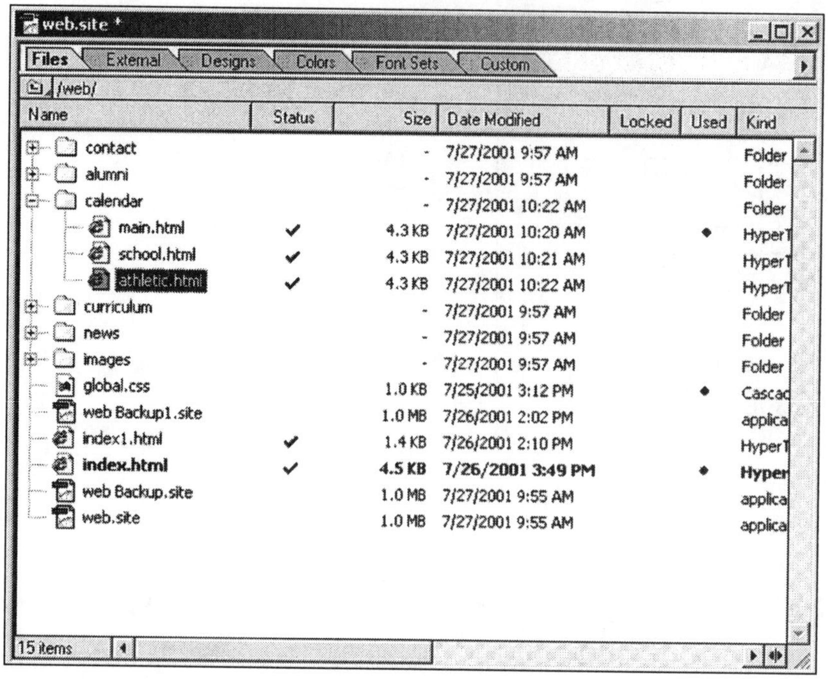

Main Page Content

9. Close the athletic.html window, and open calendar/main.html again.

10. Using your File Explorer, go to assets/calendar and open Main.doc. This file contains the text assets for your main Calendar page. Select all the text that is not part of the table (that is, everything except the two titles), copy them, and then switch back to GoLive. Replace the words Page Content with the text in your clipboard by pasting it, as shown here.

11. Now create a horizontal spacer by dragging the Line Icon ⌐ from the Objects palette to the page content cell and placing it directly in front of the first word in this cell like you did before.

12. Apply a Header 2 Style to the title Washington High - School Calendar by selecting these words and right-clicking (PC) or control-clicking (Mac) them. In the Context menu, choose Header, Header 2.

13. Assign the Header 2 Style to the second title. The result looks like this.

Washington High - School Calendar

Washington High - Athletic Calendar

14. Save your file.

First Table

15. Create a table with one cell and one row by dragging the Table Icons from the Object palette to the space below the first title (Washington High – School Calendar):

Washington High - School Calendar

Washington High - Athletic Calendar

16. You need to modify the number of cells and rows in the Table Inspector to show 1 instead of 3.

Washington High - School Calendar

Washington

| Inspector | View Controller | ► |

Table | Row | Cell

Rows 1   Columns 1
Width 64   Pixel
Height   Auto

17. In the Inspector under the Table Tab, click the Browse button to Import Text.

18. Browse to assets/calendar and select main1.txt to open it.

This file was created by exporting an Excel spreadsheet file as a tab-delimited text file. It was necessary to do this because this is the best way to import tabular data to GoLive without losing the table cell structure.

19. The result of the import will look like this.

20. Now format the table layout. Start with selecting the September cell, and on the Table Inspector under the Cell Tab, change the value of Column Span to 7.

21. Also, change the Column Span to 7 for the More cell.

22. Place your cursor in the "September" cell, switch to the Source View and paste class="Header" to the td tag (about line 86) to format the word September.

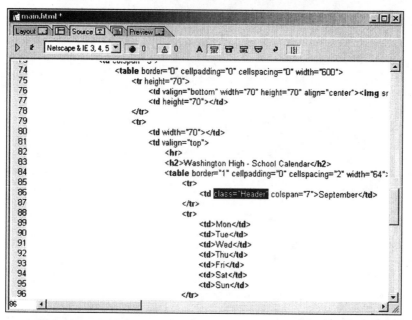

23. Switch back to Layout view. Notice that the word September has disappeared because it now has a white font color. You need to assign a background color to this cell: Right-click the cell and choose Select Cell from the Context menu. Click the color square in the Table Inspector and change the RGB value to 204,51,0.

September							
Mon	Tue	Wed	Thu	Fri		Sat	Sun
3	4	5	6	7		8	9
	"First day of school; meet in advisement rooms, 8:00 AM"	"Counselor meetings, Juniors, 1st period"		"Sports orientation: cross country and football, 3:00 PM"			
More							

24. Select the word Mon, and apply the Header 2 Style.

25. Apply the same style to all the other days in this row.

September						
Mon	Tue	Wed	Thu	Fri	Sat	Sun
3	4	5	6	7	8	9
	"First day of school; meet in advisement rooms, 8:00 AM"	"Counselor meetings, Juniors, 1st period"		"Sports orientation: cross country and football, 3:00 PM"		
More						

26. Now apply the Header 3 Style to the dates in the row beneath the day row.

September						
Mon	Tue	Wed	Thu	Fri	Sat	Sun
3	4	5	6	7	8	9
	"First day of school; meet in advisement rooms, 8:00 AM"	"Counselor meetings, Juniors, 1st period"		"Sports orientation: cross country and football, 3:00 PM"		
More						

27. Select the table. In the Inspector under the Table Tab, apply the following specifications to the table:

- Width: 490 pixels

- Cell Padding: 2

28. Save your file.

Second Table

29. Create a table with one cell and one row beneath the second title (Washington High – Athletic Calendar) and click the Browse button to Import Tab-Text. Select assets/calendar/main2.txt.

Washington High - Athletic Calendar						
September						
Mon	Tue	Wed	Thu	Fri	Sat	Sun
10	11	12	13	14	15	16
	MSBVB - St. Mark's: 5:00 (T)	GVB - ESD: 4:30/4:30 (H); FH-ESD: 4:00/5:00 (H); JV/VGVB - Hockaday: 4:30/6:00 (T)	JVFB - Temple Christian: 4:30/6:00/7:30 (H); JV/VFH - Hockaday: 5:00/6:00 (T); VFB leaves for Phoenix 3:45 pm	VBVB leaves 8:00 am for Castle Hills Tournament in San Antonio; VFB - Arizona Military Institute: 7:30 (T)	VBVB - Castle Hills Tournament in Tempe	
More						

30. Use the Table Inspector, Cell Tab to format this table and assign a column span of 7 to the top and bottom cells. Assign a cell background color of 204, 51, 0.

September						
Mon	Tue	Wed	Thu	Fri	Sat	Sun
10	11	12	13	14	15	16
	MSBVB - St. Mark's: 5:00 (T)	GVB - ESD: 4:30/4:30 (H); FH-ESD: 4:00/5:00 (H); JV/VGVB - Hockaday: 4:30/6:00 (T)	JVFB - Temple Christian: 4:30/6:00/7:30 (H); JV/VFH - Hockaday: 5:00/6:00 (T); VFB leaves for Phoenix 3:45 pm	VBVB leaves 8:00 am for Castle Hills Tournament in San Antonio; VFB - Arizona Military Institute: 7:30 (T)	VBVB - Castle Hills Tournament in Tempe	
More						

31. Assign the following styles to these items:

- "September": class="Header"–You will do this in the source code (see Step 23).

- Days of the week: Header 2

- Dates: Header 3

Your result will look like this.

September						
Mon	Tue	Wed	Thu	Fri	Sat	Sun
10	11	12	13	14	15	16
	MSBVB - St. Mark's: 5:00 (T)	GVB - ESD: 4:30/4:30 (H); FH-ESD: 4:00/5:00 (H); JV/VGVB - Hockaday: 4:30/6:00 (T)	JVFB - Temple Christian: 4:30/6:00/7:30 (H); JV/VFH - Hockaday: 5:00/6:00 (T); VFB leaves for Phoenix 3:45 pm	VBVB leaves 8:00 am for Castle Hills Tournament in San Antonio; VFB - Arizona Military Institute: 7:30 (T)	VBVB - Castle Hills Tournament in Tempe	

More

Washington High - Athletic Calendar

32. Select the complete table, and in the Inspector under the Table Tab, change the width to 490 pixels and the cell padding to 2.

33. Save your file.

34. Assign the links to the table titles and More words. Start with the first table and select the title. In the Text Inspector, create a link and point it to school.html.

Washington High - School Calendar

Inspector   View Controller

Link Style

school.html

Target

Title

September			
Mon	Tue	Wed	Tl
3	4	5	6
	"First day of	"Counselor	

35. Assign the same link to the word More at the bottom of this table.

36. Repeat Steps 34 and 35 to assign links to the next title and table. The links need to point to athletic.html.

37. Save your file, and test it in your browser.

School Page Content

38. Close main.html, and open school.html.

39. As in the previous section, select the Line Icon from the Basic Tab of the Object palette. Drag the Line Icon to the empty cell to create a horizontal spacer for the title of the table.

40. Replace Page Content with Washington High – School Calendar, and apply the Header 2 Style to it.

41. Below it, create a table with one cell and one row.

42. Select the table. In the Inspector under the Table Tab, import the file assets/calendar/school.txt to get this result.

43. Assign a column span of 7 to the September cell in the Cell Tab of the Table Inspector. Click the color box and assign a cell background color of 204, 51, 0.

44. Assign the following styles to these items:

- "September": class="Header": You will do this in the source code (see Step 23).

- Days of the week: Header 2

- Dates: Header 3

Your result looks like this.

45. Select the complete table. In the Inspector under the Table Tab, change the width to 490 pixels and the cell padding to 2.

46. Save your file.

47. To finish the school.html page, you will need to add a link back to the main calendar page. Add SCHOOL to the word CALENDAR in the subheader cell and link the word CALENDAR to main.html.

48. After having assigned the link and while CALENDAR is still highlighted, switch to the Source view and add the class identifier class="h1" after the start of the anchor tag (<a) (about line number 70).

```
69
70 '5" bgcolor="#cd3300"><a class="h1" href="main.html">CALENDAR</a>: SCHOOL</td>
71
```

49. Save your file, and look at it in your browser window. Remember to reload the browser. The upper part of your page should look like this.

Athletic Page Content

50. Close school.html, and open athletic.html.

51. After that, insert the horizontal spacer by inserting the Line Icon from the Basic Tab of the Object palette.

52. Replace Page Content with Washington High – Athletic Calendar, and apply the Header 2 Style to it.

53. Below it, create a table with one cell and one row.

54. Select the table. In the Inspector under the Table Tab, import the file assets/calendar/athletic.txt to get the following result.

Washington High - Athletic Calendar						
September						
Mon	Tue	Wed	Thu	Fri	Sat	Sun
					1	2
3	4	5	6	7	8	9
	First day of school					
10	11	12	13	14	15	16
	MSBVB - St. Mark's: 5:00 (T)	GVB - ESD: 4:30/4:30 (H); FH-ESD: 4:00/5:00 (H); JV/VGVB - Hockaday: 4:30/6:00	JVFB - Temple Christian: 4:30/6:00/7:30 (H); JV/VFH - Hockaday: 5:00/6:00 (T); VFB leaves for Phoenix 3:45 pm	VBVB leaves 8:00 am for Castle Hills Tournament in San Antonio; VFB - Arizona Military Institute:	VBVB - Castle Hills Tournament in Tempe	

55. In the Cell tab of the Table Inspector, assign a Column Span of 7 to the September cell. Change the cell color to 204, 51, 0.

56. Assign the following styles to these items:

- "September": class="Header"–You will do this in the source code (see Step 23).

- Days: Header 2

- Dates: Header 3

57. Select the complete table and in the Inspector under the Table Tab, change the width to 490 pixels and the cell padding to 2.

58. Save your file.

59. To finish the athletic.html page, you will need to add a link back to the main calendar page. Add ATHLETIC to the word CALENDAR in the subheader cell and link the word CALENDAR to main.html.

60. After having assigned the link and while CALENDAR is still highlighted, switch to the Source View and add the class identifier, class="h1", after the start of the anchor tag (<a) (about line number 70).

```
69
70 '5" bgcolor="#cd3300"><a class="h1" href="main.html">CALENDAR</a>: SCHOOL</td>
71
```

62. Save your file, and look at it in your browser window, remembering to reload. The upper part of your page should look like this.

You have now completed the Calendar section. Congratulations!

Lab 6.5: Setting Up the Curriculum Section Pages (GoLive)

Now that you have set up the Calendar section pages, it is time to create the Curriculum subsection pages and add content to these pages in order to complete the Curriculum section.

In this lab, you insert content assets like icons and text. These assets have been created for you and are now available in your web or assets folder.

1. Start by opening your site in GoLive.

2. Double-click curriculum/main.html in the web.site window to open the file.

3. Switch to the Layout View.

4. You will start by inserting the icon image in the Icon Cell on the left-hand side beneath the navigation bar. To do this, delete the word Icon and from the Basic tab in the Object palette, drag the Image Icon over to the Icon Cell.

5. In the Image Inspector, add Curriculum Icon as Alt Text. Assign an image file by clicking the Browse button and browse to web/images/icons/curriculumicon.gif.

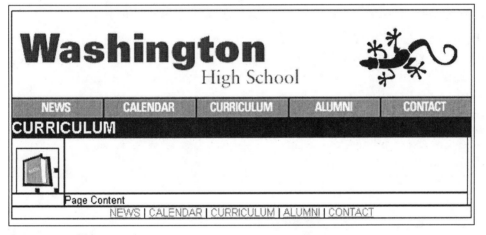

6. Save your file.

7. Create the subsection pages for your Curriculum section by saving the main.html as special.html and programs.html in your web/curriculum directory.

8. In the GoLive site window, the result looks like this.

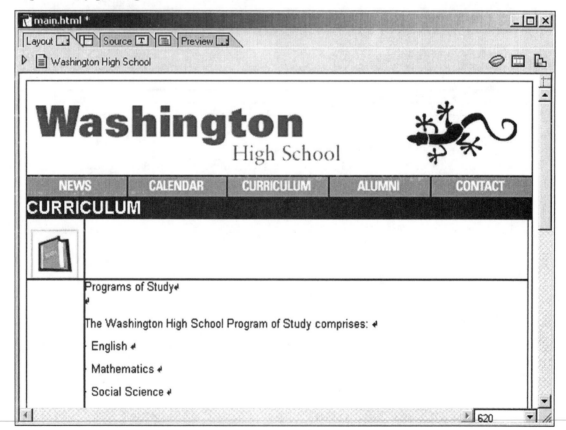

Main Page Content

9. Close the programs.html window, and open curriculum/main.html again.

10. Now by using your file explorer, go to assets/curriculum and open ain.doc. This file contains the text assets for your main page. Select all of the text, copy it, and then switch back to GoLive. Replace the words Page Content with the text in your clipboard by pasting it.

11. Create a horizontal spacer by dragging the Line icon ⬜ from the Basic Tab of the Objects palette to the page content cell and placing it directly in front of the first word in this cell like you did earlier.

12. Apply a Header 2 Style to the title Programs of Study by selecting these words and right-clicking (PC) or control-clicking (Mac) on them. In the Context menu, choose Header, Header 2.

13. Assign the Header 2 Style to the second title and delete the line breaks. The result will look like what's shown here.

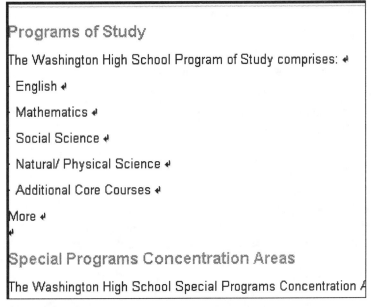

14. Save your file.

15. Delete all line breaks behind the lines.

16. Now select all bullet list items beneath the first title, and create an unnumbered list by clicking the Unnumbered List icon 🔳 in the top menu bar.

17. Delete the dots after the bullet items.

> ## Programs of Study
>
> The Washington High School Program of Study comprises:
>
> - English
> - Mathematics
> - Social Science
> - Natural/ Physical Science
> - Additional Core Courses

18. Format the second list of bullet items the same way.

> ## Special Programs Concentration Areas
>
> The Washington High School Special Programs Concentration Areas are:
>
> - Academy of Communications and Multimedia Technology
> - Academy of Design and Manufacturing Technology
> - Academy of Scientific Inquiry
> - Sport Science Academy
> - Tech Prep
> - Advanced Placement
> - Career Connection
> - Aerospace Science (Air Force Junior ROTC)

19. Assign the links to the titles and More words. Start with the first title and select the title. In the Text Inspector, create a link and point it to programs.html and assign the same link to the first More word.

> ## Programs of Study
>
> The Washington High School Program of Study comprises:
>
> - English
> - Mathematics
> - Social Science
> - Natural/ Physical Science
> - Additional Core Courses
>
> More
>
> | Inspector | View Controller | ▶ |
>
> Link | Style
>
> ∞ c/ɔ ⊚ programs.html
>
> Target

20. Now assign the links to the second title and the second More word by pointing them to special.html.

21. Save your file.

Programs Page Content

22. Close the main.html and open programs.html.

23. Now create a horizontal spacer by dragging the Line Icon ⬜ from the Basic Tab of the Objects palette to the page content cell and placing it right before the first word in this cell like you did before.

24. After that, replace Page Content with Programs of Study and apply the Header 2 Style to it.

25. Create a table with one cell and one row beneath the title. Select the table. On the Table Tag of the Text Inspector, click the Browse button to import the table data. Browse for the assets/curriculum/programs.txt file.

Programs of Study		
English	Mathematics	Social Science
Acting I	Algebra I (Level 1)	Afr-Am History
AM Literature	Algebra I / H (Level 1)	Am Government
Classical Literature	Algebra I A (.5 Units Max) (Level 1)	Am Government / H
Contemporary Literature	Algebra I B (.5 Units Max) (Level 1)	Am History
Drama I	Algebra II (Level 2)	Am History / AP

26. Use the Inspector to modify the Table width to 490 Pixel and to Cell Pad to 2.

27. Apply the Header 3 Style to the table titles in the first row.

Programs of Study		
English	Mathematics	Social Science
Acting I	Algebra I (Level 1)	Afr-Am History

28. Then apply it to the headers in row 26.

Natural/ Physical Science	Additional Core Courses	
Anatomy / Physiology (Lab)	Computer Programming I	
Anatomy / Physiology / H (Lab)	Computer Programming II	
Astronomy Solar/ Galactic (Lab)	Computer Science / AP	

29. To finish the programs.html page, you need to add a link back to the main curriculum page. Add PROGRAMS to the word CURRICULUM in the subheader cell and link the word CURRICULUM to main.html.

30. After having assigned the link and while CURRICULUM is still highlighted, switch to the Source View and add the class identifier, class="h1", after the start of the anchor tag (about line number 66).

```
65 <tr>
66      <td class="Header" colspan="5" bgcolor="#990066"><a class="h1" href="main.html">CURRICULUM</a>: PROGRAMS</td>
67 </tr>
68 <tr>
```

31. Save your file, and look at it in your browser window. Remember to reload. The upper part of your page should look like this.

Special Page Content

32. Close programs.html and open special.html.

33. Insert the horizontal spacer by inserting the Line Icon from the Basic Tab of the Objects palette.

34. Replace Page Content with Special Concentration Areas and apply the Header 2 Style to it.

35. Below it, create a table with one cell and one row.

36. Select the table. In the Inspector under the Table Tab, import the file assets/curriculum/special.txt to get this result.

Special Concentration Areas

Academy of Communications and Multimedia Technology	Academy of Design and Manufacturing Technology	Academy of Scientific Inquiry
Multimedia	Drafting and Illustrative Design	Biology
Presentations	"Technology 1, 2, 3"	Chemistry
Multimedia Technology	"Production Technology 1, 2, 3 "	Physics
Multimedia Research		Environmental Science
Computer Art		Biology for the 21st century
Computer Graphics		Chemistry (Lab)

37. Select the complete table. In the Inspector under the Table Tab, change the width to 490 pixels and the cell padding to 2.

38. Apply the Header 3 Style to the table titles in row 1, row 13, and row 25.

Special Concentration Areas

Academy of Communications and Multimedia Technology	Academy of Design and Manufacturing Technology	Academy of Scientific Inquiry
Multimedia	Drafting and Illustrative Design	Biology
Presentations	"Technology 1, 2, 3"	Chemistry
Multimedia Technology	"Production Technology 1, 2, 3 "	Physics
Multimedia Research		Environmental Science
Computer Art		Biology for the 21st century
Computer Graphics		Chemistry (Lab)
Advanced Computer Graphics		Physics (Web-based)

39. Save your file.

40. To finish the special.html page, you need to add a link back to the main curriculum page. Add SPECIAL to the word CURRICULUM in the subheader cell and link the word "CURRICULUM" to main.html.

41. After having assigned the link and while CURRICULUM is still highlighted, switch to the Source View and add the class identifier class="h1" after the start of the a tag in line number 66, as shown here.

```
65 <tr>
66     <td class="Header" colspan="5" bgcolor="#990066"><a class="h1" href="main.html">CURRICU
67 </tr>
```

42. Save your file, and look at it in your browser window: Remember to reload. The upper part of your page should look like this.

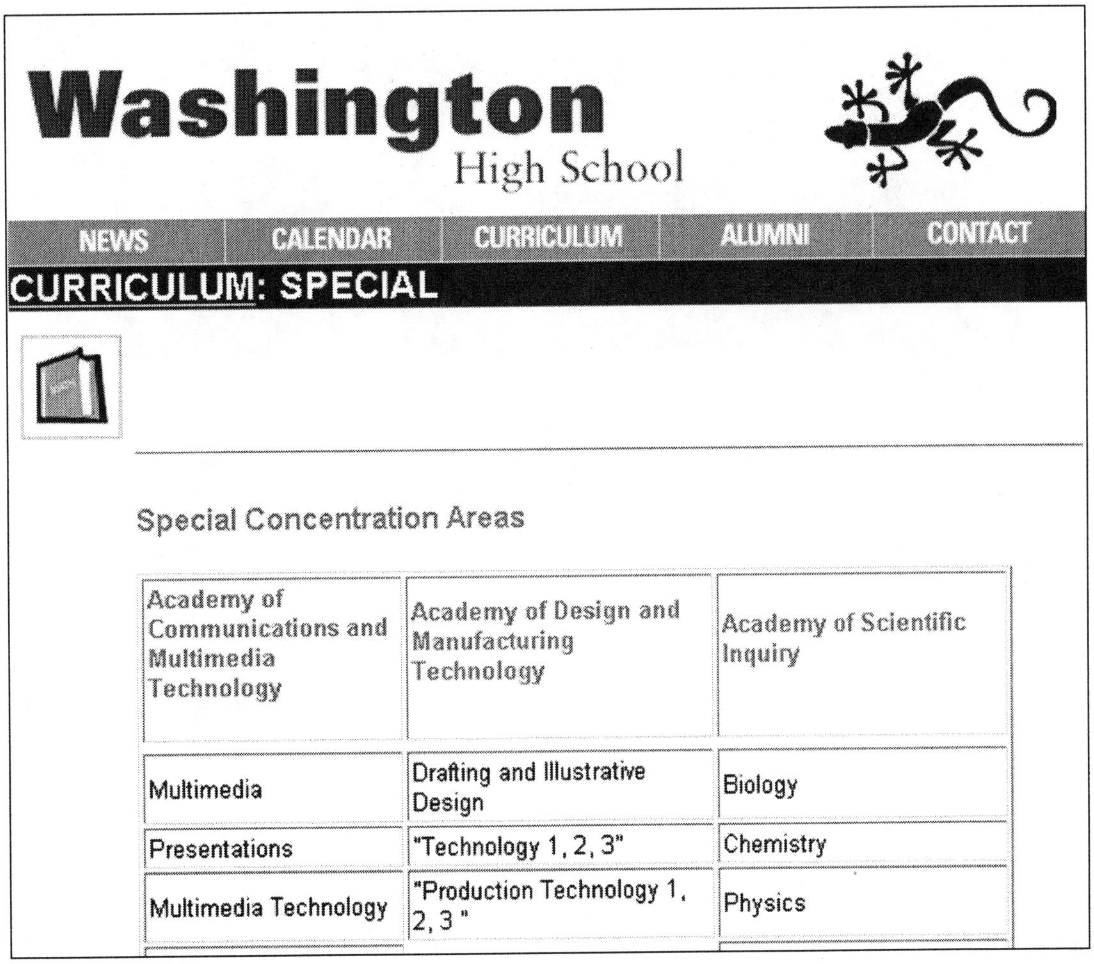

You have now completed the curriculum section. Congratulations!

Lab 6.6: Setting Up the Alumni Section Pages (GoLive)

Now that you have set up the Curriculum section pages, it is time to create the Alumni subsection pages, add content to these pages, and that complete the Alumni section setup.

In this lab, you insert content assets like icons and text. These assets have been created for you and are now available in your web or assets folder.

- Start by opening your site in GoLive.

- Double click alumni/main.html in the web.site window to open the file.

Switch to Layout view.

1. Start by inserting the Image icon from the Basic Tab of the Objects palette to the Icon Cell on the left-hand side beneath the navigation bar. Delete the word Icon.

2. In the Image Inspector, add Alumni Icon as Alt Text. Assign an image file by clicking the Browse button 🖼, and browse to web/images/icons/alumniicon.gif.

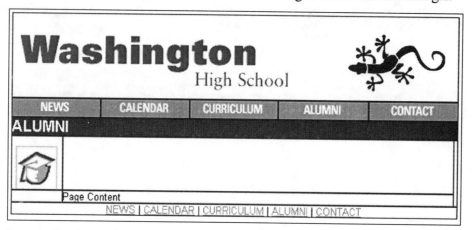

3. Insert a horizontal spacer with the Line Icon from the Basic Tab of the Objects palette before Page Content.

4. Save your file.

5. Create the subsection pages for your alumni section by saving the main.html as list.html and news.html in your web/alumni directory.

6. In the GoLive site window, the result looks like what's shown here.

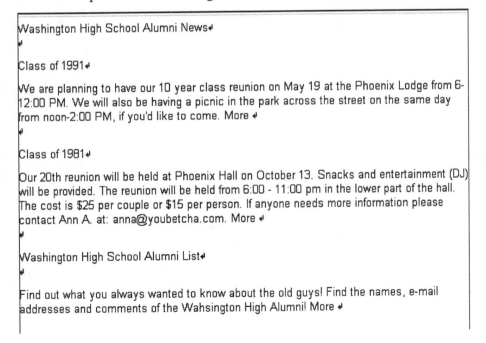

Main Page Content

7. Close the news.html window and open alumni/main.html again.

8. Using your File Explorer, go to assets/alumni and open Main.doc. This file contains the text assets for your main page. Select all the text, copy it, and switch back to GoLive. Replace the words Page Content with the text in your clipboard by pasting it.

Washington High School Alumni News↵

↵

Class of 1991↵

We are planning to have our 10 year class reunion on May 19 at the Phoenix Lodge from 6-12:00 PM. We will also be having a picnic in the park across the street on the same day from noon-2:00 PM, if you'd like to come. More ↵

↵

Class of 1981↵

Our 20th reunion will be held at Phoenix Hall on October 13. Snacks and entertainment (DJ) will be provided. The reunion will be held from 6:00 - 11:00 pm in the lower part of the hall. The cost is $25 per couple or $15 per person. If anyone needs more information please contact Ann A. at: anna@youbetcha.com. More ↵

↵

Washington High School Alumni List↵

↵

Find out what you always wanted to know about the old guys! Find the names, e-mail addresses and comments of the Wahsington High Alumni! More ↵

9. Now apply a Header 2 Style to the first title by selecting these words and right-clicking (PC) or control-clicking (Mac) on them. In the Context menu, choose Header, Header 2.

10. Assign Header 3 Styles to the subheaders.

11. Assign the Header 2 style to the second title and delete the line breaks. The result looks like this.

> **Washington High School Alumni News**
>
> **Class of 1991**
>
> We are planning to have our 10 year class reunion on May 19 at the Phoenix Lodge from 6-12:00 PM. We will also be having a picnic in the park across the street on the same day from noon-2:00 PM, if you'd like to come. More
>
> **Class of 1981**
>
> Our 20th reunion will be held at Phoenix Hall on October 13. Snacks and entertainment (DJ) will be provided. The reunion will be held from 6:00 - 11:00 pm in the lower part of the hall. The cost is $25 per couple or $15 per person. If anyone needs more information please contact Ann A. at: anna@youbetcha.com. More
>
> **Washington High School Alumni List**
>
> Find out what you always wanted to know about the old guys! Find the names, e-mail addresses and comments of the Wahsington High Alumni! More

12. Save your file.

13. Assign the links to the titles and More words. Start with the first title by selecting it. In the Text Inspector, create a link and point it to news.html and assign the same link to the first and second More words.

> **Washington High School Alumni News**
>
> Class of 1991
>
> We are planning to have our 10 year class reunion on May 19 at the Phoenix Lodge from 6-12:00 PM. We will also be having a picnic in the park across the street on the same day from noon-2:00 PM, if you'd like to come. More
>
> Class of 1981
>
> Our 20th reunion will be held at Phoenix Hall on October will be provided. The reunion will be held from 6:00 - 11:0 The cost is $25 per couple or $15 per person. If anyone contact Ann A. at: anna@youbetcha.com. More
>
> Inspector   View Controller
> Link Style
> news.html
> Target

14. Now assign the links to the second title and the More link under that section by pointing them to list.html.

Washington High School Alumni List

Find out what you always wanted to know about the old guys! Fin[...] addresses and comments of the Wahsington High Alumni! More

15. Save your file.

News Page Content

16. Close the main.html and open news.html.

17. By using your File Explorer, go to assets/alumni and open news.doc. This file contains the text assets for your news page. Select all of the text, copy it, and then switch back to GoLive. Replace the words Page Content with the text in your clipboard by pasting it.

18. After that, apply a Header 2 Style to the title by selecting these words and right-clicking (PC) or control-clicking (Mac) on them. In the Context menu, choose Header, Header 2.

19. Assign the Header 3 Style to the subheaders. Delete the line breaks. The result will look like this.

Washington High School Alumni News

Class of 1971

Our 30 year reunion will be held August 11 at the Pine River Country Club from 5:30 p.m. to 11:00 p.m. Contact Jasmine J. at 555-3684 or jasminej@righton.com for more details.

Class of 1981

Our 20th reunion will be held at Phoenix Hall on October 13. Snacks and entertainment (DJ) will be provided. The reunion will be held from 6:00 - 11:00 pm in the lower part of the hall. The cost is $25 per couple or $15 per person. If anyone needs more information please contact Ann A. at: anna@youbetcha.com.

This is also the Phoenix Community Days weekend. We are trying to contact the following classmates: Karen B., Scott D., Bill F., Lori F., Cindy G., Terrance H., Lee J., Jackie E., Randy L., Marty M., Karen & Kathy McP., Annette H., Dirk P., Scott R., and Susan T. If you know how we might contact them, please e-mail Ann A. at the above e-mail address. Also, all teachers of this class are invited to attend!

Class of 1991

We are planning to have our 10 year class reunion on May 19 at the Phoenix Lodge from 6-12:00 PM. We will also be having a picnic in the park across the street on the same day

20. To finish the news.html page, you need to add a link back to the main alumni page. Add NEWS to the word ALUMNI in the subheader cell and link the word ALUMNI to main.html.

21. After having assigned the link and while ALUMNI is still highlighted, switch to the Source View and insert the class identifier, class="h1", between the start of the anchor tag (<a) and the href attribute (about line number 70).

```
69  <tr>
70      <td class="Header" colspan="5" bgcolor="#006666"><a class="h1" href="main.html">ALUMNI<
71  </tr>
```

22. Save your file, and look at it in your browser window: Remember to reload. The upper part of your page should look like this.

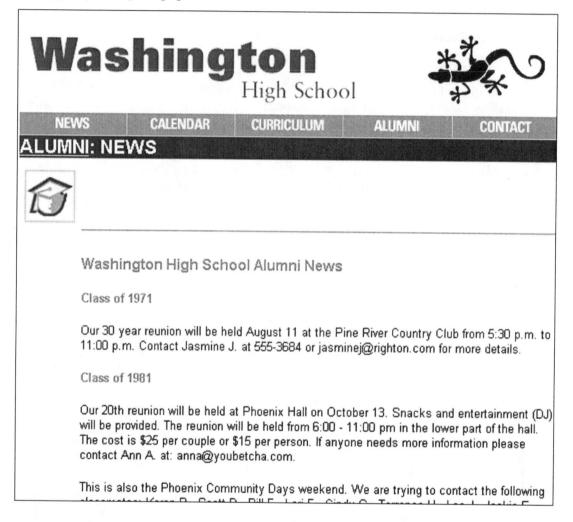

List Page Content

23. Close news.html and open list.html.

24. Replace Page Content with Washington High School Alumni List, and apply the Header 2 Style to it.

25. Below it, create a table with one cell and one row.

26. Select the table. In the Inspector under the Table Tab, import the file assets/alumni/list.txt to get the following result.

Washington High School Alumni List

Name	E-Mail	Comments
"A., Alfy"	nevermore@att2.net	I'll never forget the time Jordan let me think he had broken his foot—cast and all. That kind of sense of humor is rare these days.
		"When all the cheerleaders gave that cheer at our reunion and tried to do the "wedge"—I

27. Select the complete table. In the Inspector under the Table Tab, change the width to 490 pixels and the cell padding to 2.

28. Apply the Header 3 Style to the table titles in row 1.

29. Save your file.

30. Assign the mailto tags to the e-mail addresses listed in the middle column. To do this, select the e-mail address and copy it by pressing the keys Ctrl-C (PC) or Command-C (Mac). In the Text Inspector, assign a new link and paste the e-mail address into the field. GoLive will automatically insert the mailto.

Name	E-Mail	Comments
"A., Alfy"	nevermore@att2.net	**Inspector** View Controller ► Link Style c/⊃ mailto:nevermore@att2.n :// Target ► Title
"B., Velma"	barleycorn@excited.com	

31. Keep repeating this until all e-mail addresses are linked.

32. Save your file.

33. To finish the list.html page, you will need to add a link back to the main alumni page. Add LIST to the word ALUMNI in the subheader cell and link the word ALUMNI to main.html.

34. After having assigned the link and while ALUMNI is still highlighted, switch to the Source View and insert the class identifier `class="h1"` after the start of the anchor tag (<a) (about line number 70).

```
69 <tr>
70      <td class="Header" colspan="5" bgcolor="#006666"><a class="h1" href="main.html">ALUMNI</
71 </tr>
```

35. Save your file, and look at it in your browser window, remembering to reload. The upper part of your page should look like this.

You have now completed the Alumni section. Congratulations!

Check Your Understanding

1. What questions should an effective navigation scheme answer for users on each page of the website?

    A. Where am I? How did I get here? How do I get back?
    B. Where am I? What can I do here? How do I get back?
    C. Where am I? Where can I go from here? How do I get back?
    D. What can I do here? Where can I go from here? How do I get back?

2. What term describes the trashcan on a Macintosh desktop?

    A. Application imagery
    B. Metaphor
    C. Branding
    D. Structure

3. What is an effective use of typeface for web publications?

    A. Use at least five different font faces for each website.
    B. Use the smallest typeface that can be read on the screen.
    C. Use as much white space between lines as possible.
    D. Space characters close together.

4. What is considered a template for where elements on a web page will be placed?

    A. Information architecture
    B. Style sheets
    C. GUI
    D. Page layout

5. Which of the following is a good design practice?

    A. Scattering graphic links throughout the page
    B. Using at least 20 links per page
    C. Using the company logo as a link to the home page
    D. Having at least one 50 k image on every page

6. Which of the following statements illustrates best practices for usability?

    A. Features should not be conventional.
    B. If features are not familiar, give a detailed description of how they work.
    C. Depend on graphics to convey important navigation information.
    D. Features should be obvious and elements should work as expected.

7. Intra-page links go from one web page to another web page.

   A. True
   B. False

8. The GUI is the combination of the surface appearance and the interactive features of a web page.

   A. True
   B. False

9. What is the difference between navigation and usability in the GUI of a website?

   A. Usability defines how information is accessed. Navigation defines how easily it is accessed.
   B. Navigation defines how information is accessed. Usability defines how easily it is accessed.
   C. Navigation is more important to the interface.
   D. Usability is more important to the interface.

10. What makes text easier to read from a website?

    A. Dark-colored text on a dark image background
    B. A small typeface
    C. Short paragraphs
    D. All upper-case characters

11. Which of the following colors does not belong in the same family as the others?

    A. Neon green
    B. Orange
    C. Bright yellow
    D. Dark blue

12. Which of the following is the method for displaying type on a browser?

    A. Using HTML tags
    B. Inserting an image file containing the type
    C. Both
    D. Neither

13. All of the following are good practices EXCEPT:

    A. Respond to user action within one second.
    B. Load enough of the page so that users can start reading or navigating within 8.5 seconds.

C. Download graphics before text.

D. Warn the user beforehand that the download might be slow.

14. What is the frameset?

   A. The horizontal and vertical bars of the frame

   B. The dimensions and settings of frames

   C. The separate HTML files for each frame

   D. Term used to describe all the frames as a whole

15. A navigation element that appears on every page of the website is an example of
_____.

   A. Global navigation

   B. Parallel navigation

   C. Local navigation

   D. Remote navigation

16. A navigation element that directs the user to another place on the same web page is an example of _____.

   A. Global navigation

   B. Parallel navigation

   C. Local navigation

   D. Remote navigation

17. What is the most popular way to enhance navigation?

   A. Rollovers

   B. Image maps

   C. Scroll bars

   D. Pulldown menus

18. Which of the following is a mouseout?

   A. The button changes as the mouse passes over the image.

   B. The button changes as the mouse is clicked.

   C. The button changes after the mouse is clicked.

   D. The button changes again as the mouse leaves the image area.

19. Which is easier to set up and works faster for the user?

   A. Client-side image maps.

   B. Server-side image maps.

   C. Both are equally easy to set up.

   D. Neither is faster for the user to use.

20. What is the most visible part of the web page?

    A. Layout

    B. Style

    C. Navigation

    D. GUI

Chapter 7
Accessibility and Internationalization

Introduction

Because there are users who are disabled, it is important to understand how your design can make their access easier. A good web designer always considers accessibility issues and incorporates them into every website he or she designs. As a professional web designer, you need to do the same. In this chapter, you practice making a website accessible to disabled users and those using different browsers.

You should also consider international issues when designing websites. Today, many businesses want or need to appeal to a global audience. In this chapter, you explore how internationalization is achieved by websites for several global companies.

Focus Questions

1. Why would you create a tab order?

   _____

   _____

2. What makes image maps difficult for a disabled person to use?

   _____

   _____

3. Which type of image map is more accessible to disabled users?

   _____

   _____

4. Why is it so important to include Alt tags?

   _____

   _____

5. What does a screen reader do when it encounters an image without an Alt tag?

   _____

   _____

6. What is the role of the WAI?

   _____

   _____

7. What does the ADA require of web designers?

   _____

   _____

8. What is the best method for translating your website from English to Spanish?

   _____

   _____

9. What is Unicode?

   _____

   _____

Discovery Exercises

WAI Accessibility Checklist

Check out the latest accessibility guidelines from the W3C at www.w3.org/WAI/ Resources. Here you can find checklists that you can print out to determine whether your websites have met accessibility guidelines established by W3C. You will see that there are levels of priority. Print out all the Level 1 priorities and paste them in the remaining space on this page. Make sure that your first website satisfies the Level 1 priorities. Subsequent websites should then address Level 2 and Level 3 priorities.

Internationalization of Websites

Check out how two large global companies make websites for a variety of different countries.

For Coca-Cola

- Its U.S. website, www.coca-cola.com.

- A European website such as www.coca-cola.dk for Denmark or www.coca-cola.fr for France.

- An Asian website, such as www.cocacola.co.jp for Japan or www.coke.com.my for Malaysia.

- A website from South America, such as www.coca-cola.com.ar for Argentina or www.coca-cola.com.pe for Peru.

A Coca-Cola European Website

For which country is the website intended? _____

What language(s) is(are) displayed? _____

Is the Coca-Cola logo the same as on the U.S. website? _____

Would you recognize the brand in this country? _____

What is different about this site from the others, particularly the U.S. site? _____

_____

How is this site localized for this country? _____

_____

A Coca-Cola Asian Website

For which country is the website intended? _____

What language(s) is(are) displayed? _____

Is the Coca-Cola logo the same as on the U.S. website? _____

Would you recognize the brand in this country? _____

What is different about this site from the others, particularly the U.S. site? _____

_____

How is this site localized for this country? _____

_____

A South American Coca-Cola Website

For which country is the website intended? _____

What language(s) is(are) displayed? _____

Is the Coca-Cola logo the same as on the U.S. website? _____

Would you recognize the brand in this country? _____

What is different about this site from the others, particularly the U.S. site? _____

_____

How is this site localized for this country? _____

_____

Nike

Now check out how Nike handles internationalization. Go to the main website at www.nike.com. There, you see that the home page is divided into continents: North America, Europe, Asia, and Latin America. For North America and Asia Pacific, a few individual countries are listed, like U.S., Canada, Japan, Korea, and Taiwan. But for European and Latin American users, users choose which language to view.

Click on each of the European language websites available.

A European Nike Website

Are all the European sites basically the same website with similar layout, graphics, and information? _____

_____

An Asian Nike Website

Are all the Asian Pacific sites basically the same with similar layout, graphics, navigation scheme, and information? _____

_____

How do these sites differ from the European sites?

_____

A South American Nike Website

Are all the South American sites basically the same with similar layout, graphics, navigation scheme, and information?

_____

How do these sites differ from the European and Asian Pacific sites?

_____

How did the web designers of the Nike websites accommodate internationalization? Did they design a site for a region (for example, Latin America, Europe, Asia Pacific, North America) and then translate that site to different languages?

_____

_____

_____

_____

_____

_____

Lab 7.1: Testing Site Accessibility

"The power of the web is in its universality. Access by everyone regardless of disability is an essential aspect."

— Tim Berners-Lee, W3C Director and Inventor of the World Wide Web

So often, when we design and implement web pages, we stop before we should. That is, we sometimes fail to put our websites and their pages to tests of accessibility so that we can ensure our ability to communicate clearly to anyone, no matter their browser or their disability.

Testing for Site Accessibility

Certainly just as important as making your site viewable and functional across several representative browsers, accessibility by users with common disabilities must be aggressively pursued from the beginning of the design process.

Current statistics show that 10 to 20 percent of the population has visual, auditory, physical, or cognitive disabilities which make their access to the web difficult. Also, with the median age rising, visitors to websites may have combinations of these disabilities, making the responsibility of those building websites even more profound.

Some web designers create a "text-only" page, which screen readers such as JAWS can read aloud. Sometimes, that sort of parallel page is the best solution, depending on the requirements for the page to function and communicate. However, the following checklist suggests alternatives to such a page. It must be emphasized that the ability of your pages to communicate clearly across the broad spectrum of disabled visitors will determine the value of your site. It is a responsibility that must not go unheeded.

The following checklist is compiled from sources such as the W3C to use with your websites to ensure that your pages have a high degree of accessibility for visitors with disabilities.

The Checklist

Because screen readers help those who are visually impaired cope with web pages, it is important to give the readers as many cues as possible to get through the page:

1. Load the web page that you want to test and ensure that it is working the way you designed it to work.

   (For several of the following checkpoints, it might be helpful to turn off the graphical display of the browser.)

2. To turn off the browser's graphic display, in Internet Explorer on the PC, go to Tools, Internet Options, Advanced and uncheck the Multimedia option "Show Pictures". On the Mac, go to Edit, Preferences, Web Content. Note the ability to enable or disable plug-ins (Mac Internet Explorer 4.5 and 5.0).

3. In Netscape, options for suppressing graphics are found under Edit, Preferences.

4. Return to your page to check its functionality.

5. Ensure that all graphics important to the use of the page have descriptive Alt tags included.

6. Make sure Alt tags have descriptions that either identify the graphic or tell what will happen when you click on a graphic that is also a link.

- Example of a good Alt tag: <alt="Go to the Washington High Contact Page.">
- Example of a bad Alt tag: <"Click here.">

7. For those graphics used only for decoration, ensure that they have Alt tags that look like this: <alt="">

8. Check that these additional non-text elements have a textual alternative:

- Graphical representations of text (including symbols)
- Image map regions
- Animations (for example, animated GIFs and Flash sequences)
- Images used as list bullets
- Spacers
- Graphical buttons

9. Ensure that the Tab key provides a logical excursion through the page.

- In a page with links, the Tab key should take the user from link to link.
- Include mailto: links in the Tab order on your page, so that disabled users can contact you about your site.
- Within a form, the Tab key should take the user from field to field in a logical sequence.
- Use the tabindex tag to control the order of fields accessed via the Tab key.
- Here is an example of a tabindex assigned to a radio button:

  <input type="radio" name="Choice2" value="Chocolate"

  tabindex="4">
- Here is an example of tabindex being used with the span tag:

  <span tabindex="3">The New War</span>
- Adobe's GoLive allows the user to set up tab indexes within web pages easily.
- A general rule of thumb is to always specify a tabindex with elements that are intended to be clicked or that are important aspects of a sequence, such as an outline.

10. Use Cascading Style Sheets with the following minimal requirements:

- Use a default font size of at least 12 points for its static size. Body (Font Family: Verdana, Arial, sans-serif; font-size:12 pt)

- Use relative sizes based on the default.

  h1 (Font Size: 200%)

  h2 (Font Size: 150%)

  h3 (Font Size: 125%)

- Use em (which most browsers render as italic) for emphasized text.

- But if you wanted to have em appear in bold italic, a simple change in the CSS would look like this:

  em (Font Style: italic; Font Weight: bold)

- Avoid deprecated tags. Instead of the <font color="blue"> tag, use

  body (color: blue; background: white)

  strong (color: red)

  in the CSS.

11. Organize web pages so they can be read without style sheets. In other words, ensure that the page does not rely on the CSS to be deciphered by a screen reader. If at all possible, provide client-side image maps instead of server-side image maps. This makes it much easier for a screen reader to decipher.

    - Divide large blocks of information into more manageable groups. This is just good web writing style, but also helps visitors with visual disabilities.

    - Provide information about the general layout of a site (for example, a site map or table of contents). If you have tables on your page, identify row and column headers. Since screen readers read table cells sequentially, this is a must.

    - If you use frames, use your frameset page to title each frame to facilitate frame identification and navigation. Navigation is always a potential hazard in frames, but titling each frame enables the screen reader to more clearly follow linking between frames.

12. If you use JavaScript, ensure that pages are usable when scripting is turned off.

13. This recommendation might require a text-only alternative page, but that depends on the script. Ensure that foreground and background color combinations provide sufficient contrast when viewed by someone having color deficits.

    - Provide navigation bars to highlight the navigation scheme.

    - Create a style of presentation that is consistent across pages.

    - Referring to elements as disparate as color and navigation, this checkpoint is essential to providing smooth transitions between your pages.

    - If your page has an image map, provide redundant text links for each active region. These text links can be provided at the bottom of a page or section.

- <Alt> tags should also identify each image map region. Provide alternatives to the audio portions of your multimedia: Let Alt tags tell the story, if the story is short (256 characters is the limit).

- Provide easily accessible links to transcripts of any speech included in your pages. Provide text alternatives for these non-text elements:

    - Sounds (played with or without user interaction)

    - Standalone audio files

    - Audio tracks of video and video

- Use clear and simple language appropriate for your site's content.

14. Again, remember that if you are unable to create an equivalent page by using these guidelines, provide a link near the top of the page to an alternate page that is accessible, has equivalent information, and is updated as often as the original page.

Although this checklist is a rather challenging one, after web designers become accustomed to providing clearly accessible pages, the list becomes easier to manage.

Check Your Understanding

1. All of the following improve accessibility to a website *except*:

    A. Design for ease of comprehension

    B. Design for device dependence

    C. Proper use of markup and style sheets

    D. Providing of clear navigation mechanisms

2. What is the correct way to identify an image that is only for decoration and should be skipped by a screen reader?

    A. label=none

    B. alt=ignore

    C. alt=""

    D. label=""

3. What happens if you do not use the Alt attribute?

    A. The screen reader says "image."

    B. The screen reader skips the image.

    C. The screen reader comes to a halt.

    D. Nothing.

4. Which statement would be a best practice when designing web pages for an international audience?

    A. Always use symbols rather than words.

    B. It is better to use words than symbols.

    C. If you use symbols, make sure they are universally recognizable.

    D. Both B and C.

5. Which of the following is true regarding the ADA?

    A. Alternative information must be of equal quality as the original information.

    B. Indicate that alternative accessibility is present on the website.

    C. Explanations of how alternative accessibility is accomplished on the website.

    D. All of the above.

6. Which of the following helpful web page technologies was *not* developed for visually impaired users?

    A. Voice recognition

    B. Screen reader

    C. Screen magnifiers

    D. Screen explicators

7. Which tags would be used if you wanted a link to pages with the same information but designed for those with special needs?

   A. Title
   B. Link
   C. Body
   D. Tabindex

8. Tabs in the header of an HTML document have priority over tabs in the body of an HTML document.

   A. True
   B. False

9. Which of the following does not improve accessibility?

   A. Using style sheets
   B. Identifying links
   C. Creating a logical tab order
   D. Using a table for ease of layout

10. All symbols are global.

   A. True
   B. False

11. Why should you always use a person to translate a website from one language to another?

   A. Translation software does a literal translation.
   B. A human translator does a literal translation.
   C. A human translator promotes ambiguity.
   D. It is more economical to use a human translator.

12. From an accessibility standpoint, it is important to write clearly and simply and summarize blocks of text so screen readers will have less to read.

   A. True
   B. False

13. Which type of image map is easier for disabled users to access?

   A. Client-side.
   B. Server-side.
   C. They are both equally easy to access.
   D. Neither can be accessed by disabled users.

14. Which of the following requires that alternative information be of a quality equal to the original information?

    A. W3C
    B. WAI
    C. ADA
    D. 508

15. What is the best method for labeling a stop button on an animation?

    A. Use the red, octagonal stop sign symbol.
    B. Use the word "stop."
    C. Use the picture of a hand with its palm facing outward.
    D. Use an X.

16. Which statement is true regarding tab ordering of links?

    A. The first tab in the HTML document is the first tab accessed when using the Tab key.
    B. The last tab in the HTML document is the default tab accessed by using the Tab key.
    C. You can use the tabindex attribute to assign tab order.
    D. Tabs in the header of an HTML document have priority over tabs in the body of an HTML document.

17. Before using a symbol, make sure that it is universally recognized.

    A. True
    B. False

18. Who publishes accessibility guidelines?

    A. IETF
    B. WAI
    C. IAB
    D. ISOC

19. Which of the following would make your website easier for a disabled viewer to use?

    A. Use brighter colors for those that are colorblind.
    B. Use only black and white so that all viewers see the same thing.
    C. Create alternative pages for various types of disabilities and use link tags to get there.
    D. Use lots of sound so that a visually impaired viewer can hear what is written in text.

20. Which statement is especially important for visually impaired users of a web page?

    A. Summarize text or divide it into small blocks.

    B. Use words with fewer than 10 letters.

    C. Create web pages with long paragraphs.

    D. Provide a link to another company's website that is designed for disabled users.

Chapter 8
Media Creation

Introduction

In this chapter, you explore image formats, dimensions, and file sizes typically used on the web. These characteristics of images are important because you need to determine these characteristics for each image used on your websites. As technology changes, you might find that formats change as do the acceptable range of sizes for image files.

Lab 8.1 shows you how to use some of the filters and tools in Adobe Photoshop. You learn to use the Despeckle filter, the Dust and Scratches filter, and the Clone Stamp tool. Each can improve the photographs that you use on your websites.

Focus Questions

1. What is the software that converts printed or written characters to ASCII code?

2. What are some of the advantages of Flash animations?

3. Why should you avoid using a scanner that interpolates values?

4. What are some of the ways that you can optimize an image?

5. What can you do to reduce the download times of animations?

6. What should you consider before using an animated GIF?

7. What is one advantage of using Dynamic HTML?

8. How does streaming work?

9. What is multicasting?

10. What should you consider before using any animation or video on a web page?

Discovery Exercises

Image Formats, Dimensions, and File Sizes

Getting a feel for which formats are used for certain images, typical dimensions, and file sizes, will help you when you are optimizing images. In this exercise, you learn how to get this information and create a baseline from which you should work.

Go to www.adobe.com. If you are using Internet Explorer on the PC, right-click Adobe's logo and select Properties. If you are using Internet Explorer on the Mac, Control-click on the image. The file format, file size, and dimensions are provided.

If you are using Netscape 6.0 or later, right-click (PC) or Control-click (Mac) on Adobe's logo. Select View Image. The top bar gives you information about its format and dimensions. If the information is not displayed, go to the menu bar and choose View and then Page Info. After the window opens, maximize it. The width and height are given. To determine the image's format, look at the extension of the file. The file size is not given in Netscape Navigator.

Logo

What is the image format (GIF, JPEG, etc.) of the logo?_____

What is the size of the file in bytes? _____

What are its dimensions in pixels? _____

Now do the same for two other images on Adobe's website.

First Image

What is the image format (GIF, JPEG, etc.)? _____

What is the size of the file in bytes? _____

What are its dimensions in pixels? _____

Second Image

What is the image format (GIF, JPEG, etc.)? _____

What is the size of the file in bytes? _____

What are its dimensions in pixels? _____

Now go to the product overview pages for Adobe Photoshop at www.adobe.com/products/photoshop/overview1.html. Look at the formats for the images on the first six pages.

Adobe Photoshop Images

Which format is used for most of the photographs? _____

Are you surprised? Why? _____

_____

Why do you think that this format is used rather than the format that is normally associated with photographs? _____

_____

_____

Conclusions

What can you conclude about the use of GIF and JPEG on websites?_____

_____

Lab 8.1: Digital Image Editing (Photoshop)

This lab shows you how to remove noise, dust, scratches, and other imperfections from a digital image.

As you prepare your digital photographs for use with your website, you will need to use certain preparation techniques to remove speckles of dust (referred to as *noise*), dust, scratches, and other imperfections. Photoshop provides filters to allow your damaged photographs to be restored close to their original quality. It also provides a tool called the *Clone Stamp* that readily removes other imperfections in your photographs.

The three modules of this lab assume that you have already scanned the images you need to use for your website and that they need to be adjusted. You will start with two images: noise.tif and scratches.tif. Then, after the second graphic is resaved, you reuse it to remove a slight imperfection.

Despeckle Filter

The Despeckle filter detects the edges in a selected area of an image (where significant color changes occur) and blurs all the selection except those edges. This removes noise while preserving detail.

1. Launch Photoshop.

2. Select File, Open and choose noise.tif. *Note*: The scanned photograph is speckled with noise.

3. Because the entire photograph is affected by noise, there's no need to select a specific portion of it. In other situations, the filter can be applied only to certain areas of a photograph.

   With the Zoom tool selected, click the Fit on Screen Button (Fit On Screen) from the toolbar to zoom in on the picture.

4. From the Filter, Noise menu, select Despeckle.

5. Note the changes.

6. Because the image is adjusted to meet your needs, resave the image with a new filename.

7. Later, you will save the picture to the JPEG format by selecting File, Save for Web.

Dust and Scratches Filter

The Dust and Scratches filter reduces noise by changing dissimilar pixels. To achieve a suitable balance between sharpening the image and hiding defects, you need to try several combinations of radius and threshold settings. For finer touch-ups, this filter can be applied only on selected areas of the image.

1. If you have not already done so, launch Photoshop.

2. Select File, Open and choose scratches.tif.

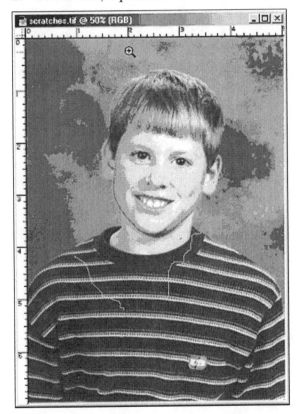

Note: The sweater has a few scratches that can be resolved by using the Dust and Scratches filter.

Use the Zoom tool 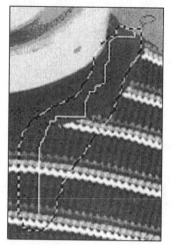 and click the image to enlarge the photo to 100 percent.

3. Select the scratched area next to the neck with the Lasso tool.

4. From the Filter, Noise menu, select the Dust and Scratches filter.

5. Adjust the Radius slider to determine how far the filter searches for differences among pixels. For this fine scratch, a radius of 1 is selected. (*Note*: Adjusting the radius upwards makes the selection blurrier, so be sure to stop at the smallest value that eliminates the defects.)

6. Adjust the Threshold slider to determine how different the pixels' values should be before they are eliminated. For this photograph, a threshold of 12 is used.

    Note the changes in the Dust & Scratches Preview screen.

7. Click OK.

8. Because some remnants of the scratches still exist, zoom in to 300 percent to make them easier to identify.

9. Deselect the area from the Lasso selection by using Ctrl-D and reselecting each of the areas with the Rectangle Marquee tool, and reapplying the Noise and Scratches filter.

    (*Note*: Rather than selecting the Dust and Scratches filter from the menu bar each time, you can use Ctrl-F as a shortcut key to the last filter you applied.)

10. Repeat Steps 4-9 to treat the other scratched area in the same manner.

11. When the image is adjusted to meet your needs, resave it with the new filename clean.tif.

12. Later, you will save the picture to the JPEG format by selecting File, Save for Web.

Clone Stamp Tool

Although not a filter, the Clone Stamp tool is often useful for removing imperfections in photographs. In this example, you're going to use the Clone Stamp tool to remove a mole from the student's picture:

1. If you have not already done so, launch Photoshop.

2. Select Open from the File menu and choose clean.tif.

3. Using the Zoom tool, magnify the area to 200 percent.

4. From the Tool Palette, select the Clone Stamp tool.

5. Check the Toolbar to make sure its Mode is set to Normal and its Opacity is set to 100 percent.

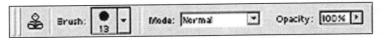

6. From the Toolbar, select a brush size that will accommodate the size of the mole. (For PC users, the brush size Hard Round 13 can been chosen. For Mac users, choose a hard brush that is approximately the same size as the mole.)

7. Holding the Alt key (PC) or Option key (Mac) down, position the brush over a portion of the neck that is free of imperfections and has similarly colored pixels.

8. Click once.

9. With the Alt key released, position the brush over the mole and click to remove it.

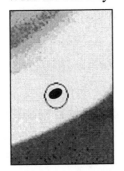

10. Note the change. Because the image is adjusted to meet your needs, resave the image with a new filename.

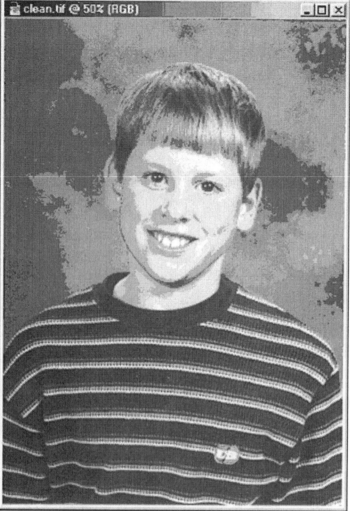

11. Go to your upper taskbar and choose File, Save for Web.

12. When the Optimized dialog box appears, choose 4-Up from the upper tab area. The first box is the original file, and the next three are available to manipulate. You can select the image by clicking inside the canvas area. The selected image will have a dark line around its canvas perimeter.

13. Go to the right side of the dialog box and click once on the Settings triangle.

14. Choose JPEG Medium.

15. Select the third image. Experiment with the different options on the right side of the Optimized dialog box, such as the quality slider. Observe the changes each one makes to your images.

16. Remember that the image selected is the one that will be saved.

17. After you optimize your image and are pleased with the results, click OK.

18. Save your new image to the appropriate folder.

Check Your Understanding

1. What is the method of playing an animation file while it is being downloaded onto the user's computer?

    A. Real-time motion
    B. Streaming media
    C. Multicasting
    D. All of the above

2. Why would you slice an image?

    A. So one area can be compressed differently from other areas to improve image quality and reduce file size
    B. To change the canvas size
    C. To resize the image
    D. To deskew the image

3. Which of the following will make web pages easier for users to scan?

    A. Long blocks of text
    B. Fewer headings
    C. Chunking
    D. Fewer lists

4. Which type of scanner passes light through a negative or slide?

    A. Transparency
    B. Flatbed
    C. Drum
    D. All of the above

5. What is a cross-platform interface for acquiring images captured by scanners and digital cameras?

    A. OCR
    B. PICT
    C. TWAIN
    D. None of the above

6. It is advisable to import the scans directly into the image-editing software for professional image scanning.

    A. True
    B. False

7. _____ is (are) a measurement of the sharpness on a computer screen; _____ is (are) also a measurement of sharpness of an image in print.

    A. DPI; PPI
    B. PPI; DPI
    C. Both DPI and PPI; DPI
    D. PPI; both DPI and PPI

8. What is a dot pitch?

    A. The angle at which characters lean
    B. The maximum number of dots per inch
    C. The darkness of the pixels
    D. The number of pixels per dot

9. If you wanted the highest quality photographs, what type of digital camera should you use?

    A. One with a charge-coupled device chip
    B. One with a complementary metal-oxide semiconductor chip
    C. One with TWAIN capability
    D. None of the above

10. What of the following are some of the kinds of formats that digital cameras take photographs in?

    A. GIF and JPEG
    B. PNG and PICT
    C. TIFF and JPEG
    D. PICT and PNG

11. Which of the following is primarily vector-based software?

    A. Adobe Photoshop
    B. Adobe Illustrator
    C. Corel Photo-Paint
    D. Macromedia Dreamweaver

12. Which type of software would you choose to manipulate images from digital cameras?

    A. Vector-based
    B. Bitmap-based
    C. TWAIN-based
    D. None of the above

13. What is the white point on a computer screen?

    A. When the red, green, and blue lights are off

    B. When the red, green, and blue lights are at full intensity

    C. The central dot on the screen that you see when turning the monitor on or off

    D. None of the above

14. Which of the following is required for slicing to decrease download of a large image?

    A. Original image is a JPEG.

    B. Always save each slice as a GIF.

    C. Save each slice using the best compression method based on that slice.

    D. Use the most number of slices as possible.

15. Why would you use Dynamic HTML?

    A. You can animate HTML text rather than creating text within an image.

    B. Users do not need special plug-ins or players

    C. You are creating animations with a single image.

    D. All of the above

16. Which file format is used for vector-based web animations?

    A. FLA

    B. GIF

    C. MOV

    D. SWF

17. How does the despeckle filter reduce noise on an image?

    A. Blurs the image

    B. Fills in the missing pixels

    C. Adjusts the brightness of neighboring pixels

    D. Interpolates the image

18. What is an advantage of using SWF animations?

    A. They can be optimized for low-bandwidth connections.

    B. They can be interactive.

    C. Audio can be embedded within them.

    D. All of the above.

19. You should always evaluate every animation used by asking these two questions: Will animation improve the delivery of information? Is the animation quick and easy for the user to download and playback?

   A. True
   B. False

20. What is the method of transmitting a file that multiple users can access at once?

   A. Real-time
   B. Streaming
   C. Multicasting
   D. Cascading

Chapter 9
Interactivity

Introduction

This chapter explores the concepts and technologies discussed in the curriculum and the *Cisco Networking Academy Program: Fundamentals of Web Design Companion Guide*, namely dynamic websites, rollover effects, and forms.

Dynamic websites create pages on demand. The data displayed on dynamic web pages is not hard-coded into the HTML page, but stored in a database. The layout is stored in a template. After a browser requests a page, the content is pulled from the database's fields and displayed in the layout template. In this chapter, you see real-life examples of dynamic websites.

Rollover buttons are the most popular way to enhance navigation. You can achieve a rollover effect with static images using JavaScript, Java, or multimedia formats like SWF files. In this chapter, you analyze code used to create rollover effects for hyperlinks.

Finally, you add examples of forms on the web to this book so that you will have a reference when you are designing forms. Lab 9.1 focuses on setting up a contact form for the course project.

Focus Questions

1. How do interactivity and animation differ?

   _____

   _____

   _____

   _____

2. What do you need to consider before using an interactive element in your design?

   _____

   _____

3. Can an animation also be interactive?

   _____

   _____

4. How does a browser display applets?

   _____

   _____

5. What do you need to create a rollover effect with static images?

   _____

   _____

6. Name two sources for a database used by a dynamic website.

_____

7. How is ciphertext decrypted into plaintext?

_____

_____

8. What are three types of VRML technologies used to simulate moving around in virtual space?

_____

_____

9. How can you use JavaScript when creating feedback or order forms?

_____

_____

10. What are SVG and SMIL? What do they require in order for them to be displayed on a user's browser?

_____

_____

_____

_____

Discovery Exercises

Rollovers

Look at the code and answer the following questions:

```
<style>
<!--
A {text-decoration:none}
A:link {color:red; text-decoration:none}
A:visited {color:green; text-decoration:none}
A:active {color:blue; text-decoration:bold}
A:hover {color:blue; text-decoration:underline}
-->
</style>
```

1. What does this code do?

   _____

   _____

   To see if you are correct, insert this code in the head portion of an HTML document that contains hyperlinks. Then preview the page in Adobe GoLive.

2. What color are unvisited hyperlinks?

   _____

3. Move your mouse over a hyperlink. What happened to the hyperlink?

   _____

4. Click that hyperlink. What happened to the hyperlink?

   _____

5. Go to another hyperlink. What happened to the first hyperlink?

   _____

Dynamic Websites

Go to an e-commerce site, such as www.llbean.com. Some dynamic websites like this one are connected to a database that lets you know whether that particular item is in stock. Check out their camping products. Choose a tent.

1. What options are you given for this tent?

   _____

2. Can you choose a color and size?

   _____

3. Can you choose the quantity of tents you want?

   _____

4. Is the tent in stock?

   _____

5. Which features of this dynamic website would you likely incorporate into an e-commerce site?

   _____

   _____

6. Which features of this dynamic website would you not be likely to incorporate into an e-commerce site?

   _____

   _____

Forms

Look for three forms that have different layouts and fields. Print them out and record each one's location for future reference.

Form 1
URL: _____

Type of form: _____

Circle features you like about this form and cross out features you do not like.

Form 2
URL: _____

Type of form: _____

Circle features you like about this form and cross out features you do not like.

Form 3

URL: _____

Type of form: _____

Circle features you like about this form and cross out features you do not like.

1. What is typically asked in a form?

   _____

   _____

2. What are some unique or unusual fields in these forms?

   _____

3. How are they laid out? Is it logical?

   _____

   _____

4. Which features would you use in future websites?

   _____

   _____

5. Which features would you avoid using in future websites?

   _____

   _____

Lab 9.1: Setting Up the Contact Section Pages (GoLive)

Now that you have set up the alumni section pages, it's time to create the contact sub-section pages and also add content to these pages. At the end of this lab, you will have completed the Contact Section. You will add an online form to allow visitors to your website to ask questions and offer comments. After the visitor completes the form, it is forwarded to the e-mail address of your choice. This lab investigates how GoLive creates and implements online forms.

In this lab, you insert content assets such as icons and text. These assets have been created for you and are now available in your web or assets folder.

1. Start by opening your site in GoLive.

2. Double-click contact/main.html in the web.site window to open the file.

3. Switch to the Layout view.

4. Start by inserting the Image icon from the Objects palette, Basic tab in the Icon Cell on the left-hand side beneath the navigation bar and delete the word Icon.

5. In the Image Inspector, add Contact Icon as Alt Text and assign an image file by clicking the Browse button 🖼 and browse to web/images/icons/contacticon.gif.

6. Insert a horizontal spacer by dragging the Line icon from the Object palette, Basic tab before Page Content.

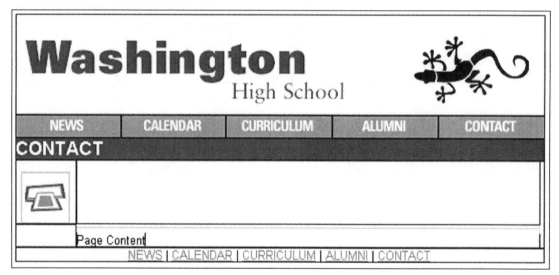

7. Save your file.

Next, you create the subsection pages for your contact section by saving the main.html as list.html and form.html in your web/contact directory.

8. In the GoLive site window, the result looks like this.

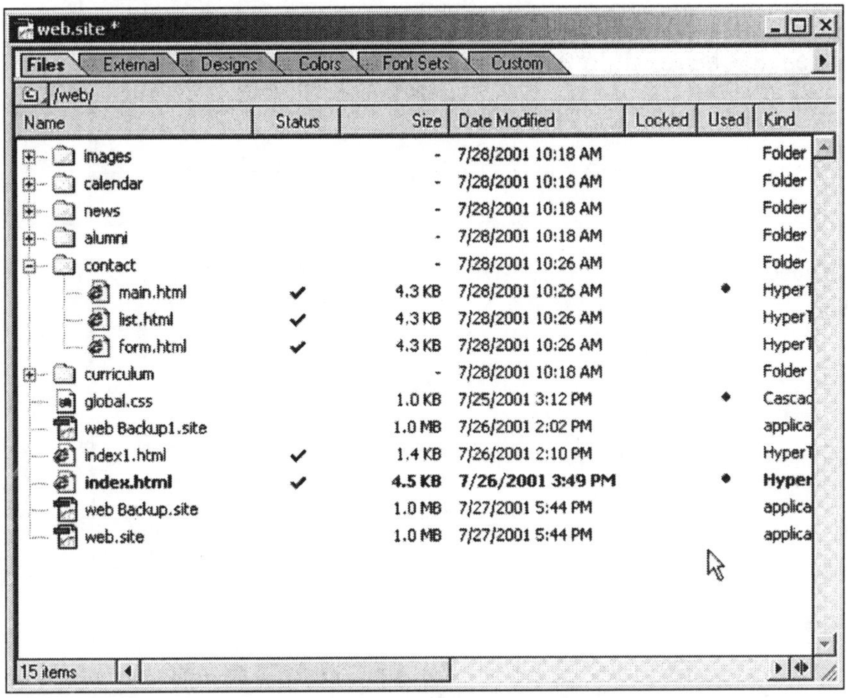

Main Page Content

9. Close the form.html window and open contact/main.html again.

10. By using your File Explorer, go to assets/contact and open main.doc. This file contains the text assets for your main page. Select all the text, copy it, and switch back to GoLive. Replace the words Page Content with the text in your clipboard by pasting it, as shown here.

11. Apply a Header 2 Style to the two titles by selecting these words and right-clicking (PC) or control-clicking (Mac) them. In the Context menu, choose Header, Header 2.

12. Delete the line breaks. The result looks like this.

Teacher List

Need to get a hold of one of your teachers? You can look them up in this teachers list! More

Contact Form

You have questions about:

- Grants

- Scholarships

- School Code

- Extracurricular Activities

- Test results

- Conferences

- College visits

- School Calendar?

Fill out this online contact form and we will get right back to you. More

13. Select all bullet list items beneath the first title, and create an unnumbered list by clicking the Unnumbered List icon in the toolbar.

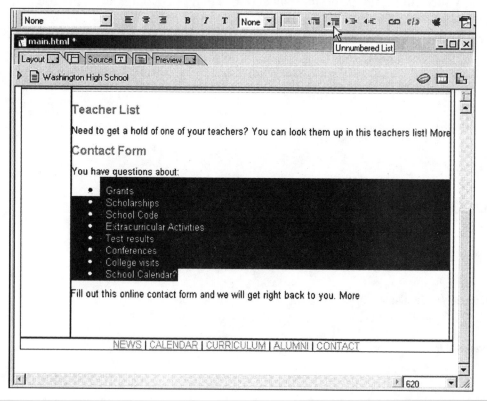

14. Delete the dots after the bullet items.

15. Save your file.

16. Now assign the links to the titles and More words. Start by selecting the first title. In the Text Inspector, create a link, point it to list.html, and assign the same link to the first and second More word.

Teacher List

Need to get a hold of one of your teachers? You can look them up in this teachers list! More

Contact Form

You have questions about:

- Grants
- Scholarships
- School Code
- Extracurricular Activities

Inspector — View Controller

Link — Style

list.html

Target

17. Assign the links to the second title and the second More word by pointing them to form.html, as shown here.

Contact Form

You have ques

- Grants
- Scholar:
- School
- Extracu
- Test res
- Confere
- College
- School

Inspector — View Controller

Link — Style

form.html

Target

Title

Fill out this onl   you. More

18. Save your file.

List Page Content

19. Close main.html, and open list.html.

20. Replace Page Content with Teacher List and apply the Header 2 Style to it.

21. Below it, create a table with one cell and one row.

22. Select the table. In the Inspector under the Table Tab, import the file assets/contact/list.txt to get this result.

Teacher List

Name	Extension	Email
"B., Bruce"	x3485	bbell@whs.k12.az.us
"B., Eileen "	x6353	ebarker@whs.k12.az.us
"B., Mary Ann "	x6350	mbelfry@whs.k12.az.us
"C., Steve "	x6250	scarper@whs.k12.az.us
"C., Patrick (Pat) "	x3344	pcornwick@whs.k12.az.us
"C., Daniel "	x3335	dcyrus@whs.k12.az.us
"D., Gary "	x6392	gdelossantos@whs.k12.az.us
"F., June "	x6382	jfarnikki@whs.k12.az.us

23. Select the complete table. In the Inspector under the Table Tab, change the width to 490 pixels and the cell padding to 2.

24. Apply the Header 3 Style to the table titles in row 1.

25. Save your file.

26. Now, you assign mailto tags to the e-mail addresses listed in the middle column. To do this, select the e-mail address and copy it by hitting the keys Ctrl-C (PC) or Command-C (Mac). Then, in the Text Inspector, assign a new link and paste the e-mail address into the field. GoLive automatically inserts the mailto.

27. Keep repeating these steps until all e-mail addresses are linked, as shown here.

Teacher List		
Name	Extension	Email
"B., Bruce"	x3485	bbell@whs.k12.az.us
"B., Eileen "	x6353	ebarker@whs.k12.az.us
"B., Mary Ann "	x6350	mbelfry@whs.k12.az.us
"C., Steve "	x6250	scarper@whs.k12.az.us
"C., Patrick (Pat) "	x3344	pcornwick@whs.k12.az.us
"C., Daniel "	x3335	dcyrus@whs.k12.az.us
"D., Gary "	x6392	gdelossantos@whs.k12.az.us
"F., June "	x6382	jfarnikki@whs.k12.az.us
"G., Joan "	x6363	jgorneault@whs.k12.az.us
"H., Kathje "	x6275	khoskins@whs.k12.az.us
"J., Gregory (Greg) "	x3328	gjourday@whs.k12.az.us
"K., Phillip "	x6309	pkletter@whs.k12.az.us

28. Save your file.

29. To finish the list.html page, you need to add a link back to the main contact page. You can do this by adding LIST to the word CONTACT in the subheader cell and linking the word CONTACT to main.html.

30. After having assigned the link and while CONTACT is still highlighted, switch to the Source View and add the class identifier, class="h1", after the start of the anchor tag (<a) (approximately line number 67).

```
66:tr>
67    <td class="Header" colspan="5" bgcolor="#666600"><a class="h1" href="main.html">CONTACT<
68:/tr>
```

31. Save your file, and look at it in your browser window, remembering to reload. The upper part of your page should look like this.

Teacher List

Name	Extension	Email
"B., Bruce"	x3485	bbell@whs.k12.az.us
"B., Eileen "	x6353	ebarker@whs.k12.az.us
"B., Mary Ann "	x6350	mbelfry@whs.k12.az.us
"C., Steve "	x6250	scarper@whs.k12.az.us
"C., Patrick (Pat) "	x3344	pcornwick@whs.k12.az.us
"C., Daniel "	x3335	dcyrus@whs.k12.az.us
"D., Gary "	x6392	gdelossantos@whs.k12.az.us
"F., June "	x6382	jfarnikki@whs.k12.az.us
"G., Joan "	x6363	jgorneault@whs.k12.az.us
"H., Kathje "	x6275	khoskins@whs.k12.az.us
"J., Gregory (Greg) "	x3328	gjourdav@whs.k12.az.us

Form Page Content

32. Close list.html and open form.html.

33. Now replace the words Page Content with this text:

```
Contact Form

Please fill out our contact form, below, and click on Send It! We will be in
contact with you shortly.

Thank you for your time and interest in Washington High School!
```

34. Apply the Header 2 Style to the title, as shown here.

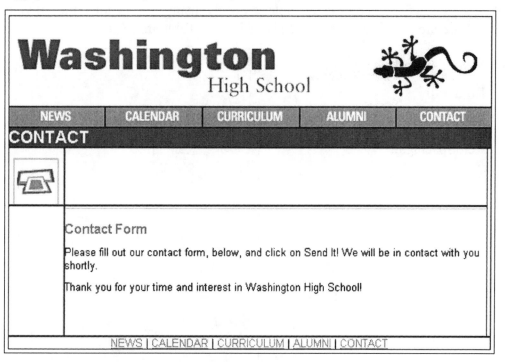

35. Go to your assets/contact folder, open form.doc, and print out the file for reference. This is the template for the form you are now creating.

36. In GoLive, select the Form Elements tab [icon] in your Objects palette. Create a form by dragging the Form icon [icon] to your form.html window and dropping it beneath the text.

[image]

37. Place a 1-column, 14-row table within the form element (click the Basic tab of the Objects palette first). You use the table to evenly display the various lines of your form. Here are the values you should have in your Table Inspector:

- Width: 490 pixels

- Border: 0

- Cell Padding: 0

- Cell Spacing: 2

38. Begin adding fields to the form by clicking in the first row of the table and typing the description of the field First Name: *. Press Shift-Enter to generate a line break. Click back to the Form tab of the Object palette, and drag a Text Field icon beneath the description. In the Form Inspector, type First_Name in the Name field, leave the Value field blank, and type 30 in the Visible characters field.

39. Arrange the remaining fields, as shown here, using the values in the table. The last field, Comments, is a text area. *Note*: Leave the Value field blank.

Field Description	Row Number	Name	Value	Visible
Last Name: *	2	Last_Name		30
Street Address: *	3	Address		30
City: *	4	City		30
State: *	5	State		15
ZIPCode: *	6	ZIP		15
Phone Number:	7	Phone		15
Fax Number:	8	Fax		15
E-Mail Address: *	9	Email		30 (Max 80)
Comments:	13	Comments		Rows: 6, Columns: 30

F

First Name: *↵

Last Name: *↵

Street Address: *↵

City: *↵

State: *↵

ZIPCode: *↵

Phone Number:↵

Fax Number:↵

E-Mail Address: *↵

Comments:↵

40. When you are finished entering fields and descriptions, click the First Name field and check the Tab option in the Form Inspector. Enter 1 in the Tab text box to indicate the first form field in the tabbing chain.

41. Click the Start/Stop Indexing button ⊞ to the right of the Tab text box. A little yellow square appears on each of the form fields. Simply click each yellow square in the order you wish your visitor to fill out the form. (The numbers in the squares should be consecutive.)

First Name: *↵
1

Last Name: *↵
2

Street Address: *↵
3

City: *↵
4

State: *↵
5

ZIPCode: *↵
6

Phone Number:↵
7

Fax Number:↵
8

E-Mail Address: *↵
9

Comments:↵
10

Inspector | View Controller ▶ | ✕

Name | Comments

Rows | 6

Columns | 30 | Wrap | Default ▼

Focus

☑ Tab | 10 | ⊞ | Key

☐ Disabled | ☐ Readonly

Content

Form Text Area

42. When you are finished, click the Indexing button again to set the tabbing chain and hide the squares.

43. In the cell below the e-mail address, type I am a: and add a line break.

44. Now in the Object Inspector with the Form tab selected, drag a Radio button icon ⊙ to this cell.

E-Mail Address: *↵

I am a:↵
○

45. In the Form Radio Button Inspector, type "status" in the group name field and "student" in the Value field. Then type Current Student in the area to the right of the radio button and add a line break.

46. Use the following table and illustration to fill in the rest of the status radio buttons and descriptions.

Radio Button Description	Group	Value
Parent	status	parent
Teacher	status	teacher
Alumni Member	status	alum
Interested Visitor	status	visitor

Each radio button belongs to the same group so your visitor can only select one option from the group.

47. Finally, click the Current Student radio button and again select the Tab option in the Form Inspector. Enter 10 in the Tab text box to indicate the 10th form field in the tabbing chain and assign indices from 10 through 14 to your radio buttons. When you're finished, click the Indexing button again to set the tabbing chain and hide the squares.

48. In the row with the Interested Visitor radio button, type "Please send me information about:" and add a line break. Now it is time to include eight check boxes with different values. When the information is sent back to you via e-mail, those values will indicate the type of information your visitor expects to receive from you.

49. Go back to the Object palette, Form tab. Choose the Checkbox icon , and drag it to the following line. Type the word Grants next to it and add a line break. Add the name grant and the value Grants to the Form Check Box Inspector.

50. Add six more checkboxes. Use the following table to add the corresponding names and values for each checkbox in the Form Checkbox Inspector.

Checkbox Name	Names	Value
Scholarships	scholar	Scholarships
School Code	code	School Code
Extracurricular Activities	extracurr	Extracurricular
Test Results	testresults	Test Results
Conferences	conf	Conferences
College Visits	collvisits	College Visits

51. Save your file.

52. In the next table line down, type Would you like to be added to our biweekly mailing list?. Then, using the techniques you learned earlier, add a radio button section with Yes and No as the choices. Make list the group name.

53. You can now assign the remaining tab indices. Start by assigning 15 to the Grants checkbox and number through 24 for the Comments text field. After you finish, click the Indexing button again to set the tabbing chain and hide the squares.

54. The last step in creating the form is to place a Submit button and a Reset button in the last row of the table. The icons from the Object palette, Form tab look like this:

and . Drag both to the last row. You might want to put two or three spaces between them, for appearance's sake.

55. Click the Submit button. You can change its value easily. Click the Label checkbox in the Form Button Inspector and type Send It! to change the text on the button.

56. Click the Reset button and do the same. Click the Label checkbox and type Start Over.

The form is in place, but will it work? Much of that question's answer depends on the arrangements you have made with your web server administrator, and might have to do with CGI scripting. You need to contact the person in charge of your web server for details.

However, a client-side solution to passing information from a form resides in the mailto: feature of HTML that you have already encountered before. You now have to add a mailto: feature to your website:

1. To assign the necessary specifications, select your form and in the Form Inspector enter the information listed:

    • Name: ContactSheet

    • Check the Action checkbox

    • Enter the following:

      "mailto:yourname@yourmailserver.com?subject=Washington School Contact Form Submission" into the action text field. *Note*: You need to insert a valid e-mail address to make the form work.

    • Method: Post

2. Now switch to the Source View and type enctype="text/plain at the end of the form tag (about row 83).

```
82
83 ?subject=Washington School Contact Form Submission" method="post" enctype="text/plain">
84
```

3. You have now completed the contact page setup. Save your file.

Contact Form Validation

After your contact page is in place and working properly, it's a good idea to add some basic JavaScript to your form in order to verify that your visitors are filling in your page appropriately. For example, it would be useless to have a visitor fill out a form but neglect to include her/his e-mail address if that is the primary way you plan to make contact. You will now add the necessary JavaScript code and identification to enable a form validation.

1. Make sure that you are still in the Source View Source T.

2. Scroll toward the Head portion at the top of the page.

3. You can see that the script tag has already been inserted while you created the rollover navigation buttons.

4. Scroll down until you see the end of the mouseover script at row 48.

5. Place your cursor in this row and press Enter a couple of times. Then paste the following code from this document in place:

```
<!-- Original: wsabstract.com -->
function checkrequired(which) {
var pass=true;
if (document.images) {
for (i=0;i<which.length;i++) {
var tempobj=which.elements[i];
if (tempobj.name.substring(0,8)=="required") {
if (((tempobj.type=="text"||tempobj.type=="textarea")&&
tempobj.value=='')||(tempobj.type.toString().charAt(0)=="s"&&
tempobj.selectedIndex==0)) {
pass=false;
break;
        }
      }
   }
}
if (!pass) {
shortFieldName=tempobj.name.substring(8,30).toUpperCase();
alert("Please make sure the "+shortFieldName+" field is properly
completed.");
return false;
}
else
return true;
}
```

6. Make sure not to delete the existing end comment // --> tag before the end script tag: It is essential for the correct functioning of the scripts.

```
form.html

Layout   Source   Preview

▷  ✦  Netscape & IE 3, 4, 5 ▼   ● 0   ⚠ 0   A  SRC  URL  ↵  |↓|

53 if (document.images) {
54 for (i=0;i<which.length;i++) {
55 var tempobj=which.elements[i];
56 if (tempobj.name.substring(0,8)=="required") {
57 if ((((tempobj.type=="text"||tempobj.type=="textarea")&&
58 tempobj.value=="")||(tempobj.type.toString().charAt(0)=="s"&&
59 tempobj.selectedIndex==0)) {
60 pass=false;
61 break;
62        }
63      }
64    }
65 }
66 if (!pass) {
67 shortFieldName=tempobj.name.substring(8,30).toUpperCase();
68 alert("Please make sure the "+shortFieldName+" field is properly completed.");
69 return false;
70 }
71 else
72 return true;
73 }
74
75 // -->
76 </script>
113    ◄
```

Now, scroll to approximately row 109 where the form tag is inserted. At the end of the form tag, place the following statement on one line: onSubmit="return checkrequired(this).

```
108
109 intact Form Submission" method="post" enctype="text/plain" onSubmit="return checkrequired(this)">
110
```

7. Save your file.

8. Now you need to assign which fields will be validated to make sure that they were filled out. The script you inserted does the validation, but it needs to be told which form elements to validate. Adding a name value, starting with required, to the form element tag identifies these elements.

9. Select the First Name field in the Layout View and add "required" to the front of the current Name field.

| First Name: * |
| Last Name: * |
| Street Address: * |

Inspector / View Controller

— Properties

Name: requiredFirst_Name

10. In case you haven't noticed, all required fields are indicated with a *. To make this apparent to the user also, add this text at the bottom of your form: * Required Fields.

11. Continue to add the "required" identifier in front of the name for each text field in the Form Text Field Inspector (Last Name, Address, City, State, Zip, e-mail).

12. Check out your new form by saving it to your web folder and launching it in your web browser. Test it by leaving blank a field that you have required. When you click Submit (Send It!), an alert box should come up on your screen, informing you that the field must be properly completed.

Note

To actually send the form out you must enter a valid e-mail address: To do this, refer to Step 1.

---

13. Finally, you need to add a link back to the main contact page. Do this by adding : FORM to the word CONTACT in the subheader cell and linking the word "CONTACT" to main.html.

14. After having assigned the link, and while CONTACT is still highlighted, switch to the Source View and add the class identifier "class="h1"" after the start of the anchor tag (<a) (about line number 93).

```
92:tr>
93    <td class="Header" colspan="5" bgcolor="#666600"><a class="h1" href="main.html">CONTACT<
94:/tr>
```

15. Save your file and look at it in your browser window, remembering to reload. The upper part of your page should look like this.

Contact Form

Please fill out our contact form, below, and click on Send It! We will be in contact with you shortly.

Thank you for your time and interest in Washington High School!

First Name: *

Last Name: *

Congratulations! You just completed the Contact section of the website.

Check Your Understanding

1. Which web technology allows the user to interact with others in a 3D environment?

    A. IPIX

    B. QuickTime

    C. VRML

    D. Web3D

2. Which type of technology do both SVG and SMIL use?

    A. XML

    B. XHTML

    C. Dynamic XHTML

    D. VRML

3. What do SVG and SWF have in common?

    A. Both are vector-based.

    B. Both are capable of presenting 3D panoramas.

    C. Both are capable of supporting video and audio.

    D. Neither requires a plug-in.

4. Why is it better to use a feedback form than a mailto feature?

    A. Mailto features are unreliable.

    B. Feedback forms are read by spammers' spiders.

    C. Feedback forms can return organized information to the client.

    D. Feedback forms ensure that the user is not entering false information.

5. Which of the following is an example of an event handler triggered by a user action?

    A. Clicking the mouse button

    B. Moving the mouse over a button

    C. Submitting a form

    D. All of the above

6. What is an advantage of using applets?

    A. Small in size

    B. Highly secure

    C. Platform-specific

    D. Both small in size and highly secure

7. The data displayed on a static web page is not hard coded into the HTML page, but stored in a database and the layout is stored in a template.

   A. True
   B. False

8. What would you use to personalize a website?

   A. JavaScript
   B. VRMLScript
   C. CGI scripts
   D. Java applets

9. Which type of website creates pages by demand?

   A. XML
   B. XHTML
   C. Dynamic
   D. Static

10. Which format is used to create most rich media ads?

    A. SVG
    B. SMIL
    C. SWF
    D. JAVA

11. Which type of security feature is composed of the name of the company, the company's public key, a serial number, and an expiration date?

    A. Digital certificate
    B. Ciphertext
    C. Public key
    D. Private key

12. What is plain text?

    A. Text that is within a digital envelope
    B. Uni-encoded text
    C. Encrypted data
    D. Unencrypted data

13. Which of the following transforms data by using a key to make the data incomprehensible to all except its intended receivers?

    A. Uni-encoded
    B. Unencryption
    C. Cryptography
    D. All of the above

14. How do you add audio and video to a QuickTime animation or movie?

    A. Add them to a web page as an embedded link.

    B. Incorporate them within the QuickTime file.

    C. Write scripts for them within the QuickTime file.

    D. QuickTime cannot support audio and video.

15. Which of the following statements is correct?

    A. JavaScript is interpreted by the web server.

    B. JavaScript is a client-side script.

    C. JavaScript is a little program executed from within a browser.

    D. The ability to process JavaScript event handlers is dependent on the user enabling the virtual Java machine in the browser.

16. What is the best reason for using an interactive element?

    A. To fill up a web page

    B. To add different types of elements to your website

    C. To enable the user to interact with the site

    D. All of the above

17. The layout of a dynamic web page is stored in a template.

    A. True

    B. False

18. Where is the data stored for dynamic web pages?

    A. Frameset

    B. Database

    C. Data table

    D. Head section of the HTML document

19. Which technique helps to line up the input fields within a form?

    A. Using frames

    B. Using a table

    C. Using server-side scripts

    D. None of the above

20. What is an avatar?

    A. Virtual person

    B. Server-side script

    C. Applet

    D. 3D room or panorama

Chapter 10
Testing and Optimization

Introduction

It is important when building a new website to check the entire site for consistency and functionality. You will need to carefully go through every page, link, button, form field, and image. Errors and problems reflect poorly on you as a web designer. In this chapter, you perform a site check on a website.

It is also important to validate your HTML code to catch any mistakes that you might have made. There are programs available to validate code from those built in to WYSIWYG editors to those found on the Internet. You search for validators so that you will have them available when you begin designing sites in the future.

The lab in this chapter focuses on setting up the home page for the Washington High School project. The home page pulls all the main sections of the website together, and is the interface that most users see when coming to the site. You use Adobe GoLive to set up the home page.

Focus Questions

1. What is a validator?

   _____

   _____

2. Why would you use a validator?

   _____

   _____

3. What is the most important concept that you should remember about usability testing?

   _____

   _____

4. Explain why it is better to test three people multiple times than 10 people just once.

   _____

   _____

   _____

5. Why should you always provide width and height attributes for images?

   _____

   _____

6. What are some of the things you should be looking for when performing a site-wide consistency check?

   _____

   _____

   _____

7. What are some of the things you can do to keep the site fresh?

   _____

   _____

   _____

8. What is a cached image?

   _____

   _____

9. What is an interlaced image?

   _____

   _____

10. When is the best time to perform a usability test?

   _____

   _____

Discovery Exercises

Site Check

In this exercise, you practice checking sites for consistency, errors, and functionality. Use your personal website, if you have one, the course project website, or one of your favorite websites.

Home Page

1. How long does it take to download?

   _____

2. How are navigation buttons grouped?

   _____

   _____

3. Did all images load?

   _____

4. Did any multimedia (animations, audio, or video) load improperly?

   _____

5. Are there any broken links?

   _____

6. Are the graphics suited to the message and intention of the site?

   _____

7. Does the text have a voice matching this message?

   _____

8. Is Alt text used for images?

   _____

9. Are there spelling errors in text, buttons, or captions?

   _____

Main Section Page

Now click one of the links that takes you to a main section.

10. Is the overall tone of this page similar to that of the home page?

_____

11. Is it easy to tell where you are in the website?

_____

12. Is there a link to the home page that is easy to find?

_____

13. Are there spelling errors in text, buttons, or captions?

_____

_____

Other Pages

Now go deeper into the website.

14. Are the navigation buttons or links in the same place on every page?

_____

15. Is there a link to the home page on every page?

_____

16. Are links to other pages broken?

_____

17. Are links to other websites broken?

_____

18. Is the content current?

_____

_____

19. Do rollovers, check boxes, and radio buttons work?

_____

20. Does the search feature help you find information?

_____

_____

21. Do you get any error messages?

_____

_____

22. Are there spelling errors in text, buttons, or captions?

_____

_____

Overall Website

23. Is the design consistent throughout the site?

_____

_____

24. What could be improved?

_____

_____

Code Validators

Use a search engine and search for the keywords "HTML code validator" to find code validators on the Internet for future reference. If you have a personal website, run your code through one of the free validators.

First Validator

Company name: _____

URL: _____

What is the cost? _____

Second Validator

Company name: _____

URL: _____

What is the cost? _____

Third Validator

Company name: _____

URL: _____

What is the cost? _____

Fourth Validator

Company name: _____

URL: _____

What is the cost? _____

Fifth Validator

Company name: _____

URL: _____

What is the cost? _____

Lab 10.1: Setting Up the Home Page (GoLive)

Now that you set up all the section pages, it's time to complete the home page and add the final assets to its template. In this lab, you insert content assets, such as icons and text. These assets have been created for you and are now available in your web or assets folder.

1. Start by opening your site in GoLive.

2. Double-click contact/main.html in the web.site window to open the file.

3. Switch to Layout View.

4. Start by inserting the icon images in their respective cells. Start with the Announce ment icon on the left. Delete the words Announcement Icon and drag over an image object from the Object palette to take its place.

5. In the Image Inspector, add Announcement Icon as Alt Text. Assign an image file by clicking on the Browse button, 🖼 and browse to web/images/icons/ announcementicon.gif.

6. Insert the horizontal spacer–the Line object from the Object palette–in place of the words Horizontal Spacer.

7. You can now insert all the other image placeholders using the Image icon from the Object palette. In the Image Inspector for each, enter the Alt text and assign the image:

- News icon (web/images/icons/newsicon.gif): "News"

- Alumni icon (web/images/icons/alumniicon.gif): "Alumni"

- Calendar icon (web/images/icons/calendaricon.gif): "Calendar"

- Curriculum icon (web/images/icons/curriculumicon.gif): "Curriculum"

- Contact icon (web/images/icons/contacticon.gif): "Contact"

The Calendar, Curriculum, and Contact icons go in the same cell. Separate them by pressing Enter after they have been inserted.

8. Make sure that all icons are centered by selecting an icon and clicking the Center button.

9. Check to make sure that the icons are vertically aligned to the top of the cell. If not, you need to change the Vertical Alignment for each icon to Top.

10. Now paste the text assets. Open the file index.doc from your assets folder. Select the first two lines and copy and paste them to replace the Announcement Text. Select the Announcement Text cell, and in the Text Inspector, make sure the vertical alignment is middle.

11. Delete all extra line breaks and spaces at the end of the text. Add a line break (Shift-Enter) after the word "Lizards!"

12. Save your file.

13. Now copy the Washington High School News section and paste it into the appropriate cell by deleting the placeholder text. Apply Header 2 Style to the title and Header 3 Style to the subtitle. Delete all line breaks.

14. Copy the text from Washington High School Alumni News and paste it into the correct cell. Again, apply Header 2 and 3 Styles and delete the line breaks.

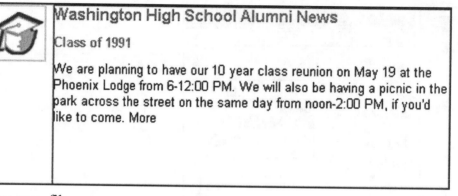

15. Save your file.

16. Select the Calendar icon, press the right arrow key once, and create a paragraph break by pressing Enter. Repeat this for the Curriculum and Contact icons.

17. In index.doc, copy the calendar text and paste it beneath the Calendar icon. Repeat this for the two other icons.

18. Select the Calendar icon and switch to the Source View. In row 99, you see the start of the td tag. Here, you need to paste this code snippet: class="hometable". This defines the cell text's font size.

```
98   <td valign="top" rowspan="2">Ver. Spacer</td>
99   <td class="hometable" valign="top" rowspan="2">
100      <div align="center">
101         <img src="images/icons/calendaricon.gif" width="54"
```

19. Your result looks like this in Layout View.

20. Bold the words Calendar, Curriculum, and Contact by using the Bold button on the toolbar.

21. Save your file.

22. Drag an Image icon from the Objects palette in the cell Vertical Spacer and delete these words. In the Image Inspector, assign the image to web/images/pixel.gif and assign a width of 2 pixels and a height of 400 pixels.

23. Now, set the properties of the table. Select one of the cells in the table, such as the news text or news icon cell. In the Inspector, switch from the Cell tab to the Table tab. In the Table tab, modify the Cell Padding and Spacing properties to 2.

24. Assign a width of 140 pixels to the Calendar/Curriculum/Contact Cell.

25. Finally, create links to the icons, titles, and More words. Use the following table as a guide.

Table 10-1: Linking Items in the Website

Item to Be Linked	Link
News icon	news/main.html
News title	
News text More	
Alumni icon	alumni/main.html
Alumni title	
Alumni text More	
Calendar icon	calendar/main.html
Calendar text	
Curriculum icon	curriculum/main.html
Curriculum text	
Contact icon	contact/main.html
Contact text	

Your result should look like this.

26. Save your file, and take a look at it in your browser (remember to reload). The upper part should look like this.

Congratulations! You have just completed your Washington High School website! It is now ready to be published.

Check Your Understanding

1. What are you checking for when you test whether a site's images are well suited to represent the site's goal, the tone of the text is consistent throughout, and page layouts are related to one another?

   A. Structure
   B. Consistency
   C. Validation
   D. Stickiness

2. What should be included in a usability test for a website?

   A. A flowchart of the website
   B. Just the website
   C. Description of the client
   D. Only web-savvy participants

3. What type of test subject should you recruit?

   A. Potential target audience.
   B. Experienced web users.
   C. Inexperienced web users.
   D. All of the above can be used.

4. What kind of sites would you monitor if your client sells computer accessories online?

   A. Other sites selling computer accessories
   B. Computer manufacturers
   C. Both
   D. Neither

5. JPEG uses _____ compression; GIF uses _____ compression.

   A. Lossless; lossless
   B. Lossless; lossy
   C. Lossy; lossless
   D. Lossy; lossy

6. What is an effective trick to decrease page-loading time for a website?

   A. Put all images in <div> layers.
   B. Use the same images on several pages.
   C. Use the height and width attributes for the images to make the images smaller.
   D. Use WYSIWYG-generated code instead of hand-coded HTML.

7. You only need to test your site on the latest versions of the two most popular browsers.

   A. True
   B. False

8. What gives the user an idea of what the image will look?

   A. An interlaced image
   B. The alt attribute for the <img> tag
   C. An animated GIF with the first frame set to zero delay
   D. An image contained in the <img lores > tag

9. When should usability testing take place?

   A. After the site is uploaded to the web.
   B. Throughout the development process.
   C. Near the end of the development process.
   D. Usability testing is not necessary.

10. Why is it better to test fewer people multiple times?

    A. Testing is more likely done throughout the design process.
    B. Three people likely will encounter the most significant problems.
    C. They are likely to encounter a new set of problems on subsequent tests.
    D. All of the above.

11. What is the advantage of including the width and height attributes in your image tags?

    A. The rest of the page can continue to load while the image is downloading.
    B. It is the preferred method to resize image files.
    C. It is required by a user needing a screen reader to browse your page.
    D. Height and width attributes are only required for animated GIFs.

12. If you do not use a validator, HTML code mistakes will display in the user's browser.

    A. True
    B. False

13. On which of the following should you test your website?

    A. Most popular browsers only.
    B. Latest browser versions only.
    C. Most popular platform only.
    D. None of the above: Test on different browsers, versions, and platforms.

14. What should be part of the recruiting process when planning a usability test?

    A. An information session that describes the function of the website

    B. Budgeting for some form of payment for each participant

    C. Finding test subjects who do not know the web designer(s)

    D. Finding test subjects who are web savvy

15. What should you check body copy, labels, headlines, and buttons for?

    A. Correct meta tags

    B. Missing Alt tags

    C. Non-validated fields

    D. Spelling and punctuation errors

16. When should a site check take place?

    A. After the site is completed

    B. At the same time as the usability test

    C. During construction of the site

    D. During the planning phase

17. What is a common result of using a site content-management scheme that involves moving pages and replacing them with more up-to-date pages with different names?

    A. Pages must be hand coded to include updated Meta content.

    B. The users will not be able to access the site from their bookmarks.

    C. The pages will not have a title.

    D. Users will be able to view the most current content from the page.

18. What is the most important concept in usability testing?

    A. Test as many people as possible.

    B. Test often.

    C. Use an experienced usability expert.

    D. Test only after the website is completed.

19. What should you use to check your HTML code for errors?

    A. DOM

    B. Validator

    C. Link manager

    D. WYSIWYG editor

20. Which of the following minimizes download time for web pages?

    A. Reusing image files throughout the website

    B. Using CSS

    C. Reducing HTML code

    D. All of the above

Chapter 11
Implementation and Hosting

Introduction

This chapter focuses on advertising and publishing your website. You explore how web rings link similar sites in order to bring new users to your site. Banners are the most popular form of advertising. You can create banners to place on other websites. You can pay to have them displayed or join a banner exchange, where you agree to host banners from other websites in exchange for placing banners on theirs. In this chapter, you learn about the types of banners that are considered acceptable by investigating the guidelines established by the leading organization dedicated to Internet advertising.

Lab 11.1 is the final lab for the course project. You learn how to publish the website by using Adobe GoLive.

Focus Questions

1. Why should the client provide a privacy policy on her website when collecting user data?

    _____

    _____

2. What information should you include in the privacy policy?

    _____

    _____

3. What is the difference between a copyright and a trademark?

    _____

    _____

4. What is co-locating?

    _____

    _____

5. What services does a co-locating service usually offer?

    _____

    _____

6. What criteria do most search engines use to rank websites?

    _____

    _____

7. What does SSL use to secure data when transmitting across the Internet?

_____

_____

8. What is a web ring?

_____

_____

9. What are some of the disadvantages of using banner exchanges?

_____

_____

10. What is co-branding?

_____

_____

Discovery Exercises

Banners

You need to familiarize yourself with the design, sizes, and types of media currently used in banners.

The *Interactive Advertising Bureau (IAB)* is the industry's leading interactive advertising association. It publishes guidelines for web advertising including those for banners, rich media, and pop-ups. Go to its website at www.iab.net/. Click the link to the rich media guidelines.

Click the links to the different types of rich media ads such as the rollover expand banner, the click expand banner, pop-ups #1 and #2, and the transitional ad.

1. Which of these rich media ads have you encountered while using the Internet?

   _____

   _____

2. Which one have you encountered frequently?

   _____

   _____

Rich Media Banners

3. What are the dimensions of the standard rich media banner?

   _____

   _____

4. What is the maximum file size for a rich media banner?

   _____

   _____

5. What are the guidelines for rollover expands for a rich media banner?

   _____

   _____

6. What are the guidelines for click expands for a rich media banner?

   _____

   _____

7. What are the guidelines for using audio and video in a rich media banner?

   _____

   _____

Rich Media Pop-Ups

8. What are the dimensions of rich media pop-up #1?

    _____

9. What are the dimensions of rich media pop-up #2?

    _____

10. What is the maximum file size for rich media pop-up #1?

    _____

11. What is the maximum file size for rich media pop-up #2?

    _____

Interstitial or Transitional Ads

12. Where do these ads appear?

    _____

    _____

13. What is the maximum file size of a transitional ad?

    _____

14. What are the dimensions of a transitional ad?

    _____

Banner Sizes

Now go to the ad unit guidelines at www.iab.net/iab_banner_standards/
bannersource.html. Here, you can see samples of the sizes of ads that are standard in the
industry. Go to the web page that shows those for banners and buttons.

15. List the names and sizes of banners and buttons that you can use.

    _____

    _____

    _____

    _____

    _____

    _____

    _____

16. Draw these buttons to size in the space below, or print out the page from the IAB site and paste it into this space.

Web Rings

A *web ring* is a free form of advertising for your website. For clients with small advertising budgets, this method could be ideal for promoting the site. There are several major drawbacks, however, to using web rings. The advertisements placed on your site could be distracting, clash with your site's design, or even draw users away from your site.

Go to dir.webring.yahoo.com/rw to see the web ring service run by Yahoo!. Here, you can join, search, or create a web ring.

Click the major category Business and Finance. Now select Home Business. You can see a list of hundreds of web rings specifically for home businesses. Each listing tells you how many sites participate in the ring. Choose a ring that has more than 50 sites. You will see a list of all the websites within that ring along with a short description of that site.

Now go back to the main categories of web rings and choose a main category.

17. Which main category did you choose?

_____

18. Which subcategory did you choose?

_____

19. What is the most popular web ring?

_____

20. How many sites are within the most popular web ring?

_____

21. What are the advantages of joining a popular web ring?

_____

_____

22. What are the disadvantages of joining a popular web ring?

_____

_____

23. What are the advantages of joining a small web ring (fewer than 10 sites)?

_____

_____

24. What are the disadvantages of joining a small web ring (fewer than 10 sites)?

_____

_____

Lab 11.1: Publishing the Site (GoLive)

Considering the number of steps preceding the publication of a website, you might wonder sometimes if you will ever be done. The answer to that question is complicated, because of the following reasons:

- As a web designer, you must be committed to providing up-to-date information on a regular basis, according to the contract you have signed with your client. In the case of the Washington High School website, you and your design team must be committed to informing your audience (students, teachers, parents, relatives, and others) about upcoming events, and those events change constantly in high school.

- There will be times in the lifespan of a site when the entire site will be reworked or redesigned and you will be, in effect, almost starting over.

Your responsibilities for launching a site to the web are threefold:

- Ensure that the site is ready for publication.

- Arrange for Web space and a connection to the server that will host the Web space.

- Publish (upload) the site.

Ensuring that the Site Is Ready for Publication

One of your foremost responsibilities prior to publication is checking for errors. It is important to check for spelling and grammatical errors as well as errors in logic in your writing.

You are also responsible for checking for errors in links between pages as well as external links from your site to other Internet sites.

One way to check for broken links is to save your site to your local hard drive (which hopefully you have been doing all along). Start your browser and open your home page (index.html). By visiting each page individually, check all of your links to make sure they are working.

GoLive also provides a feature that checks broken links for you.

Check External Links

1. Make sure you are connected to the Internet.

2. Bring up your site in GoLive.

3. Click the External tab in the Site window.

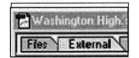

4. From the Site menu, choose Check External Links.

5. Any broken links will show the Bug icon in the Status column next to the referenced link.

Check Page Links

1. Click the Files tab in the Site window. Broken links will be indicated by the Link Warning button.

2. To correct this link error, double-click to bring up the file.

3. Reveal the Inspector (press Ctrl-1, if necessary).

4. On the Toolbar, click the Link Warnings button.

5. A red outline appears around any broken links.

6. Click the link.

7. Correct the link in the link field in the Inspector and press Enter.

8. The red box disappears, which indicates that the link is no longer empty.

9. Resave the page.

   For more information about testing and verifying links, please check GoLive's comprehensive Help–either by pressing F1 or from the menu item Help.

Arranging for Web Space and Connecting to the Server

Usually, arranging for web space takes you in one of two directions:

- Your school has already secured web space and has FTP services.

- You need to use a remote Internet service provider (ISP).

If your school already has web space secured, you will need to contact your web server administrator for details on connecting to it. Usually, each website you design and publish will have its own folder (or set of folders), along with a username and a password your administrator provides. By using the username and password, you are assured of at least a base level of security when uploading your site.

File Transfer Protocol (FTP) is the most common method by which you will connect to your web space, once it is ready. The following example takes you step by step through connecting to a site using FTP.

Free Web Space

Several web servers on the Internet allow their users free web space in return for an occasional pop-up ad appearing on their pages.

Publishing (Uploading) Your Site

You need to use the information you have received from your instructor regarding a web space that has been provided for your site.

You will need the following:

- URL: www.yourschool.edu

- FTP server location: www.yourschool.edu

- FTP server username: You

- FTP server password: *****

Although you could use a third-party FTP program, such as WS_FTP, CuteFTP, or Fetch, to move your site's files from its local hard drive to a web server, GoLive has its own FTP services built in. We will use GoLive's FTP option to connect to our school's FTP server in order to upload the site.

1. Launch your Washington High School website in GoLive.

2. Choose Settings from the Site menu.

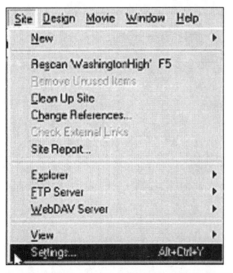

3. In the Settings dialog box, click FTP and WebDAV Server on the left and type in the FTP values you have received from your instructor (*Note*: Don't use the values shown here; they are just an example).

Some items to note:

- The values you type in depend on the configuration that you have set up for your own web space.

- The password appears in asterisks as an additional security precaution.

- Clicking in the Save checkbox maintains your password so you do not have to type it in each time. However, if you are sharing a computer, you might want to leave the Save checkbox unchecked.

- Port 21 is usually reserved for FTP access, but there are some exceptions. Be sure to check with your web administrator for details.

- Passive mode ensures that you will be able to use FTP even through most firewalls.

4. Click OK when you are done filling in your FTP configuration values.

5. On the Toolbar, click the Upload button.

6. Your cursor turns into an hourglass for the time it takes to connect.

7. Once connected, your FTP window reveals the root directory of your site, along with any additional folders your web administrator requires. A CGI folder might appear, which the web server provides by default. It is where server-based scripts that can be used with your site would be stored.

On the Toolbar, just to the right of the FTP Server connect/disconnect button, you can find the Incremental Upload button.

Note

An incremental upload refers to updating your site only with files that have changed since the last upload. Because all your files are new to this web space, the Incremental method is appropriate to use.

8. Click the Incremental Upload button. Note the values in the Upload options dialog box that appears.

9. Click OK.

Upload Options

Honor Publish state of
☑ Groups
☑ Pages

☑ Upload referenced files only

☑ Show list of files to upload

☐ Don't show again

Set as default   OK   Cancel

10. The Upload site dialog box appears with a listing of each file that is to be published. Investigate the files listed, and eliminate any files that should not be uploaded by clicking the ☑ next to the filename to deselect it.

11. Click OK to start the upload.

Uploading files...

Files remaining to be uploaded   25

/images/prostudies-header.gif

Stop

12. After the upload is complete, launch your favorite browser and point it to your new website's URL.

13. Check all pages to ensure that they have published properly. If some have not been, try republishing them again by using the Incremental method.

14. To disconnect from your FTP server after all files are published, right click in your FTP window and select Disconnect.

Congratulations! You have just published your Washington High School site!

Check Your Understanding

1. What is the exclusive ownership interest in an artistic or literary work?

    A. Copyright
    B. Patent
    C. Trademark
    D. None of the above

2. Which law has been broken if an image is reproduced without permission on a website?

    A. Trademark
    B. Copyright
    C. Ownership
    D. Free speech

3. Which of these page elements can be used by search engines to rank web pages?

    A. Content of the text, Meta tag keywords, and page title
    B. Content of images, page generator type, and Meta tag keywords
    C. Operating system of the server, domain name, and scripting type
    D. Page generator type, meta tag description, and file extension

4. Which law has been broken if a new image is created that is nearly identical to an existing logo?

    A. Patent
    B. Copyright
    C. Trademark
    D. Free speech

5. Which of the following will help determine the ranking of your site by search engines?

    A. Alt attributes
    B. Keywords
    C. Filenames
    D. All of the above

6. To test for website accessibility, you should not turn off images, scripts, animations, audio, and video.

    A. True
    B. False

7. What is the term for a company that houses a client's web server?

   A. Co-hosting
   B. Co-housing
   C. Co-locating
   D. None of the above

8. What are cookies?

   A. Configuration files used by plug-ins
   B. Items placed throughout a site to lead visitors to items of interest
   C. Small files that are placed on a user's hard drive by websites
   D. An inexpensive and easy means of securing a website

9. What are some free or inexpensive ways to market a website?

   A. Web rings
   B. Banner exchanges
   C. E-mail signatures
   D. All of the above

10. Which governmental regulations require that websites obtain "verifiable parental consent" before engaging in ongoing communications with children?

    A. COPPA
    B. ICWMA
    C. PCOM
    D. WPCA

11. What protocol does a web server use when a client browser requests a file?

    A. HTTP
    B. FTP
    C. Both HTTP and FTP
    D. Neither HTTP nor FTP

12. Both the user's browser and the web server must support SSL in order for it to work.

    A. True
    B. False

13. What is the term for when two companies partner with each other to create one site?

    A. Co-locating
    B. Co-hosting
    C. Co-housing
    D. Co-branding

14. Joe quoted a couple of lines from an article for his website and cited the author and publisher. Which of the following statements is correct?

    A. Joe has plagiarized the article.
    B. This is an example of "fair use" of the material.
    C. Joe did not need to cite the author or publisher of the article.
    D. Joe must pay for the article.

15. Which type of web-hosting solution are you recommending to a client if the recommendation includes hiring a full-time server administrator by the client?

    A. Remote hosted
    B. Co-locating
    C. In-house
    D. ISP

16. TRUSTe is a U.S. government agency that establishes guidelines to ensure children's privacy on the Internet.

    A. True
    B. False

17. What is the term for paying by how many times an ad is displayed each month?

    A. CPM
    B. Click-through
    C. Page impressions
    D. None of the above

18. Which top-level domain should be chosen for a nonprofit organization in the United States?

    A. .com
    B. .edu
    C. .org
    D. .npo

19. Which newer top-level domain is being used as an alternative to .com in the United States?

    A. .com2
    B. .biz
    C. .bus
    D. .net

20. A website that is loaded with videos and animation needs an Internet connection capable of plenty of bandwidth.

    A. True
    B. False

Chapter 12
Portfolio Development

Introduction

A *portfolio* showcases your work for a potential employer or client. Many design programs at universities and graphic design schools also require applicants to submit a portfolio.

Lab 12.1 shows you how to collect material for your portfolio, prioritize that material, and prepare it.

Focus Questions

1. What is a portfolio?

   _____

   _____

2. Which type of portfolio is essential for all web designers?

   _____

   _____

3. What are leave-behinds?

   _____

   _____

4. What should you bring to an interview to leave with the potential employer or client?

   _____

   _____

5. Why is a program like Adobe Acrobat useful on your web-based portfolio site?

   _____

   _____

   _____

6. What should you consider when choosing samples of your work for your portfolio?

   _____

   _____

   _____

7. What characteristics are important when designing your web-based portfolio?

_____

_____

_____

8. What is some of the information that should be included in your resume?

_____

_____

_____

9. What kind of samples should you include in your portfolio?

_____

_____

_____

10. After you have been invited for an interview, what should you do to prepare?

_____

_____

_____

Discovery Exercise

Check out Adobe Studio's ePortfolio at studio.adobe.com/explore/eportfolio/main.html. Here, you can view web portfolios of web designers. This is a valuable resource for seeing what other web designers are doing. You can also post your own web-based portfolio for free.

Look at the portfolios of a number of designers. Write down the name of the designers you like and what you liked about their work.

Table 12-1: Web Designer Portfolios

Designer Last Name, First Name	What I Liked About Their Work
1.	
2.	
3.	
4.	
5.	
6.	

Designer **Last Name, First Name**	**What I Liked About Their Work**
7.	
8.	
9.	
10.	
11.	
12.	
13.	
14.	

Designer Last Name, First Name	What I Liked About Their Work
15.	
16.	
17.	

Lab 12.1: Collecting Portfolio Material

When applying for a web design or production position, it is necessary to have a URL and a web-based portfolio. Even if you are applying for a graphic design position, a prospective client wants to see that you can utilize such resources as the web. It is also important to have a companion print-based portfolio that you can bring to interviews.

Often the most difficult part of creating a portfolio is deciding which material should be included. In this lab, you learn how to rate your work, determine the audience, determine the site you will post your portfolio on, and prepare each piece.

Rating Your Work

Possibly the best way to start the selection process is to gather your best samples, perhaps eight to ten from each project, in a work area and invite comment and criticism from other designers, teachers, fellow students, and colleagues. Because you have not established how you will organize the items, you might want to arrange them by type (for example, print, writing, web pages, etc.). Any "review committee" you choose will be able to make more useful remarks if they have more than one piece to compare.

This is not a time to be hard on yourself, but a time to get a frank appraisal of your work. Be sure to tell your panel that they are helping you decide on items to display in your portfolio. It might also be helpful to have a rubric for your panel to follow so they can score your items according to the same criteria. For example, you might want to have them score your work on its visual appeal, its use of color, or its clarity of message. Look at Table 12-2 and please rate each art sample on a scale from 1 to 5, with 5 being the best.

Table 12-2: Sample Rubric

	Art Sample #1	Art Sample #2	Art Sample #3	Art Sample #4
Visual Appeal				
Use of color				
Clarity of message				
Totals				

If you have essays, news, or feature articles, the rubric may contain a rating for organization, syntax, and colorful or appealing language. Use Table 12-3 to rate each writing sample on a scale from 1 to 5, with 5 being the best.

Table 12-3: Sample Rubric

	Writing Sample #1	Writing Sample #2	Writing Sample #3	Writing Sample #4
Organization				
Syntax				
Language				
Totals				

Your web designs can be assessed on organization, visual appeal, use of consistent color schemes, and clear and consistent navigation. Use Table 12-4 to rate each sample on a scale from 1 to 5, with 5 being the best.

Table 12-4: Sample Rubric

	Web Sample #1	Web Sample #2	Web Sample #3	Web Sample #4
Organization				
Visual Appeal				
Navigation				
Totals				

Samples to Include

After the scoring is complete and the results are tabulated, you will probably have a better idea of which potential portfolio items you will want to include. Be sure to:

- Select at least two items from each type of work.

- Note the items that are related to one another.

- Note as well those items that will require additional explanation.

- Begin to visualize how the items you have selected will be ordered in your portfolio presentation.

Additional Documents

An important aspect of this assembly of materials involves the context you provide with the pieces you include. In other words, it is your responsibility to provide additional documents that answer the what, when, where, and why of each piece.

For example:

"This logo was made for the introduction of the new art gallery at Washington High School last spring. It appears on the letterhead and brochures that the gallery produces, shows the diversity of the activities available at the school, and identifies immediately with the great student body."

Other documents you might want to include are additional appraisals of your work by noted or respected individuals as well as any awards your work has received.

Determining Your Audience

Another factor that will determine the pieces you select will be the audience. There are two distinct audience groups you need to consider.

One is the prospective employer to whom you will present your portfolio. You will select different pieces designing a website for an accounting firm than you will if you are designing a website for a rock band. Know the nature of your audience and plan your pieces accordingly.

Another determining group will be the audience to whom the prospective employer markets his products. Knowing or at least making an educated guess at this audience will once again influence the pieces you include in a portfolio. Ask company representatives, analyze brochures or other print media the company distributes, and check out the company's current website, if one exists.

Because color and layout are some of the first things an employer looks at when viewing your portfolio, plan at least two possible groups of pieces you will use when applying for jobs. For example, include conservative pieces when applying for a more traditional employer and be ready to replace those with your bright, animation-driven pieces when you are interviewing with a more cutting-edge company.

Determining the Type of Portfolio Site

Although you might not know the nature of the end product you will design, you should certainly approach the submission of a portfolio presentation with some ideas in mind. Producing three or four mock-ups of various site designs and being ready to explain them may give you a real advantage during interviews.

These proposed website templates could be in the form of sketches or actual web pages that you present. They could come from previous websites you have designed. Or they could take advantage of the other art and article pieces in your portfolio. This last method of assembling the portfolio pieces into a unified whole that results in a website mock-up will also demonstrate your ability as a designer to build a unified site from various assets.

Preparing the Pieces

After you determine the grouping of the various components of your portfolio, you must decide how they need to be prepared:

- If the art is in the print format (drawings, paintings, etc.), it may need to be matted. If the pieces are large, you might be better served by photographing them and presenting them in a professionally laid out album or binder.

- If they are text samples, be sure to have them neatly organized and printed in a format that is easy to read with ample margins and clear fonts.

- If any of the textual pieces have appeared with photography or designs that are also yours, be sure to include that format as well.

- If the pieces are previously designed websites, you may be served well by showing some printed representative pages from each as well as a flowchart that explains their connection to one another.

- If any of your portfolio's websites are published, be sure to include the notation that "The entire site can be viewed at www.mysite.com."

Check Your Understanding

1. Do not include plug-ins on your electronic portfolios. Clients should have them installed on their computers or they can download them if needed.

   A. True
   B. False

2. Which application converts web pages into the format PDF so they can be printed?

   A. Adobe GoLive
   B. Adobe Atmosphere
   C. Adobe Acrobat
   D. Adobe Premiere

3. When leaving a paper-based portfolio behind after an interview, always include your contact address in it so that it can be returned to you.

   A. True
   B. False

4. Which of the following practices make your portfolio easier for the interviewer to review?

   A. An organized, error-free portfolio
   B. A portfolio with a limited number of samples
   C. A portfolio that contains brief descriptions of each sample
   D. All of the above

5. Which of the following best reflects the process of designing a portfolio?

   1. Create resume and descriptions of each sample.
   2. Assemble.
   3. Determine contents.
   4. Gather and organize material.

   A. 1, 2, 3, 4
   B. 3, 1, 4, 2
   C. 3, 1, 2, 4
   D. 4, 3, 1, 2

6. Which element of your portfolio is tailored to individual clients or employers?

    A. Cover letter
    B. Resume
    C. References
    D. Both A and B

7. Which of the following statements are important for a good interview?

    A. Be prepared.
    B. Arrive early.
    C. Be positive.
    D. All of the above.

8. Which of the following are methods for marketing your web-based portfolio?

    A. Register your URL at search engines.
    B. Use an online tracking service.
    C. Both A and B.
    D. Neither A nor B.

9. If you do not have your own website to post a portfolio and do not want advertising banners appearing on your portfolio, what is you best option?

    A. Buy space on a portfolio website like portfolios.com.
    B. Use free web page builder sites like angelfire.com.
    C. Use free online community portals like geocities.com.
    D. All of the above.

10. What section of your resume should contain information about your knowledge of software, hardware, and programming languages?

    A. Experience
    B. Career Summary
    C. Skill Sets
    D. Objectives Statement

Appendix A
Check Your Understanding Answer Key

Chapter 1	Chapter 2	Chapter 3	Chapter 4
1. B	1. B	1. A	1. B
2. A	2. A	2. C	2. D
3. C	3. B	3. D	3. A
4. D	4. B	4. D	4. C
5. B	5. B	5. C	5. D
6. C	6. C	6. D	6. D
7. A	7. B	7. C	7. A
8. C	8. B	8. B	8. D
9. C	9. C	9. C	9. A
10. D	10. C	10. A	10. C
11. A	11. A	11. B	11. B
12. A	12. B	12. D	12. A
13. B	13. C	13. D	13. D
14. D	14. B	14. B	14. B
15. C	15. B	15. C	15. A
16. B	16. A	16. A	16. A
17. B	17. A	17. B	17. D
18. A	18. A	18. B	18. D
19. D	19. C	19. D	19. A
20. B	20. A	20. A	20. C

Chapter 5	Chapter 6	Chapter 7	Chapter 8
1. A	1. C	1. B	1. B
2. C	2. B	2. C	2. A
3. D	3. C	3. A	3. C
4. A	4. D	4. D	4. A
5. A	5. C	5. D	5. C
6. D	6. D	6. D	6. A
7. C	7. B	7. B	7. C
8. B	8. A	8. B	8. B
9. C	9. B	9. D	9. A
10. A	10. C	10. B	10. C
11. A	11. D	11. A	11. B
12. D	12. C	12. A	12. B
13. A	13. C	13. A	13. B
14. A	14. B	14. C	14. C
15. C	15. A	15. B	15. D
16. A	16. C	16. C	16. D
17. B	17. A	17. A	17. A
18. C	18. D	18. B	18. D
19. A	19. A	19. C	19. A
20. B	20. D	20. A	20. C

Chapter 9	Chapter 10	Chapter 11	Chapter 12
1. C	1. B	1. A	1. B
2. A	2. B	2. B	2. C
3. A	3. D	3. A	3. A
4. C	4. C	4. C	4. D
5. D	5. C	5. D	5. B
6. D	6. B	6. B	6. D
7. B	7. B	7. C	7. D
8. C	8. A	8. C	8. C
9. C	9. B	9. D	9. A
10. C	10. D	10. A	10. C
11. A	11. A	11. A	
12. D	12. A	12. A	
13. C	13. D	13. D	
14. B	14. B	14. B	
15. B	15. D	15. C	
16. C	16. C	16. B	
17. A	17. B	17. A	
18. B	18. B	18. C	
19. B	19. B	19. B	
20. A	20. D	20. A	

Notes

Notes

Notes

Notes